AF299644

CATALOGUE

OF

THE LIBRARY

OF THE LATE

REV. JAMES SUMNER,

INCUMBENT OF SHRIGLEY, NEAR MACCLESFIELD;

TO WHICH ARE ADDED

OTHER SMALL PROPERTIES;

COMPRISING

THEOLOGICAL LITERATURE

AND

STANDARD WORKS IN VARIOUS LANGUAGES,

INCLUDING

FROISSART'S CHRONICLES, by JOHNES, 13 vols. LODGE'S PORTRAITS, 12 vols. JOWETT'S EPISTLES OF ST. PAUL, 2 vols. BRYDGES' CENSURA LITERARIA, 10 vols. JAMIESON'S SCOTTISH DICTIONARY, with Supplement, 4 vols. HOUBRAKEN'S HEADS. GALLERIA PITTI, 8 vols. *morocco extra*. ALISON'S EUROPE, 21 vols. And numerous other VALUABLE PUBLICATIONS IN GREEK, LATIN, FRENCH, GERMAN, SPANISH, ITALIAN, ENGLISH AND THE ORIENTAL DIALECTS.

WHICH WILL BE SOLD BY AUCTION,

BY MESSRS.

SOTHEBY, WILKINSON & HODGE,

Auctioneers of Literary Property & Works illustrative of the Fine Arts,

AT THEIR HOUSE, No. 13, WELLINGTON STREET, STRAND, W.C.

On THURSDAY, 19th DECEMBER, 1878, & Two following Days,

AT ONE O'CLOCK PRECISELY.

May be Viewed Two Days prior, and Catalogues had.

DRYDEN PRESS: J. Davy and Sons, 137, Long Acre.

CONDITIONS OF SALE.

I. The highest bidder to be the buyer; and if any dispute arise between bidders, the lot so disputed shall be immediately put up again, provided the Auctioneer cannot decide the said dispute.

II. No person to advance less than 6*d*; above five shillings, 1*s*.; above five pounds, 2*s*. 6*d*.; and so on.

III. In the case of lots upon which there is a reserve, the Auctioneer shall have the right to bid on behalf of the Seller.

IV. The purchasers to give in their names and places of abode, and to pay down 10*s*. in the pound, if required, in part payment of the purchase-money; in default of which the lot or lots purchased to be immediately put up again and resold.

V. The lots to be taken away at the buyer's expense immediately after the conclusion of the sale; in default of which Messrs. SOTHEBY, WILKINSON & HODGE will not hold themselves responsible if lost, stolen, damaged, or otherwise destroyed, but they will be left at the sole risk of the purchaser. If, at the expiration of ONE WEEK after the conclusion of the sale, the books or other property are not cleared or paid for, they will then be catalogued for immediate sale, and the expenses the same as if re-sold, will be added to the amount at which the books were bought. Messrs. SOTHEBY, WILKINSON and HODGE will have the option of reselling the lots uncleared either by public or private sale without any notice being given to the defaulter.

VI. All the books are presumed to be perfect unless otherwise expressed; but if upon collating, any should prove defective, the purchaser will be at liberty to take or reject them, provided they are returned within ONE WEEK after the conclusion of the sale, when the purchase-money will be returned.

VII. The sale of any book or books is not to be set aside on account of any stained or short leaves of text or plates, want of list of plates, or on account of the publication of any subsequent volume, supplement, appendix or plates. All the manuscripts, autographs, all magazines and reviews, all books in lots, and all tracts in lots or volumes, will be sold with all faults, imperfections, and errors of description. The sale of any illustrated book, lot of prints or drawings is not to be set aside on account of any error in the enumeration of the numbers stated, or error of description.

VIII. No IMPERFECT BOOK will be taken back, unless a note accompanies each book, stating its imperfections, with the number of lot and date of the sale at which the same was purchased.

IX. To prevent inaccuracy in the delivery, and inconvenience in the settlement of the purchases, no lot can on any account be removed during the time of sale.

X. Upon failure of complying with the above Conditions, the money required and deposited in part of payment shall be forfeited; and *if any loss is sustained in the reselling of such lots as are not cleared or paid for, all charges on such re-sale shall be made good by the defaulters at this sale.*

Gentlemen who cannot attend the Sale may have their Commissions faithfully executed by their humble servants,

SOTHEBY, WILKINSON & HODGE,
Wellington Street, Strand.

CATALOGUE

OF

THE LIBRARY

OF THE LATE

REV. JAMES SUMNER,

INCUMBENT OF SHRIGLEY, NEAR MACCLESFIELD.

FIRST DAY'S SALE.

OCTAVO ET INFRA.

LOT
1 Barth (T. C.) Bible Manual   1865
2 Rutherford (S.) Religious Letters—Moseley (H.) Astro-Theology, 1847; and others   (48)
3 Cowper (W.) Works, with Life, &c. by R. Southey, 15 vol. *portraits and plates (spotted)*   1836-7
4 Fletcher (Rev. J.) Works, 8 vol. *portrait*   1836-8
5 Bridges (C.) Christian Ministry, 1830—James (J. A.) Pastoral Addresses—Nicholls (B. E.) Help to the Reading of the Bible, 1847; and others   (14)
6 Roberts (A.) Plain Sermons, *two series*, 4 vol. 1841-2—Short Sermons for Family Reading, by J. W. Burgon, &c. *first and second series*, 4 vol. 1865-7—McCausland (D.) Sermons in Stones, 1856; &c.   (12)
7 Bengelii (J. A.) Gnomon Novi Testamenti   1855
8 Hemans (F.) Poems, *portrait*   1849
9 Trench (R. C.) Synonyms of the New Testament, *two series, Camb.* 1854—Prayer Book, *interleaved, ib.* 1866—Alford (H.) The Year of Prayer, 1866; &c.   (10)
10 Smith (W.) Student's Gibbon, 100 *engravings*, 1857—Smith (J. T.) Streets of London, 1849—Russell's Modern Europe, by G. Townsend, 1858; &c.   (6)

B

11 Smiles (S.) Self Help, 1860—McCausland (D.) Adam and
    the Adamite, *map*, 1864—Candlish (R. S.) The Atone-
    ment, 1861; &c. (7)
12 Keble (J.) Christian Year, *Oxford*, 1836—Usher (J.) Ser-
    mons—Hall (Bp. J.) Select Devotional Works; and
    others (66)
13 Pike (J. G.) Guide for Young Disciples—Visit to the
    British Museum, *numerous illustrations*, 1838; and
    others (60)
14 Sedgwick (A.) Greek Prose Composition, 1876 — Denison
    (E. B.) Astronomy without Mathematics, 1867 — Bain
    (A.) English Composition and Rhetoric, 1869 — Mayor
    (J. B.) Greek for Beginners, 1869; &c. (13)
15 Smith (W.) First Latin Dictionary, 1862 — Curtius (G.)
    Smaller Greek Grammar, 1866; and other School
    Books (50)
16 Conway (W.) Pastoral Discourses, 1864—Carr (A.) Notes
    on St. Luke, 1875—Stillingfleet (E.) Doctrines and
    Practices of the Church of Rome, *Edinb.* 1845; and
    others (27)
17 Hare (A. W.) Sermons to a Country Congregation, 2 vol.
    portrait, 1838—Heber (Bp. R.) Parish Sermons, 2 vol.
    1839—Cooper (E.) Practical and Familiar Sermons,
    7 vol. 1830—Sketches of Sermons, 8 vol. 1833; &c. (19)
18 Bautain (M.) Art of Extempore Speaking, 1859—Sherwood
    (Mrs.) Infant's Progress, *front.* 1847—Pascal (B.)
    Provincial Letters, *Edinb.* 1851; &c. (30)
19 Evans (R. W.) Ministry of the Body, 1847 — Bishopric of
    Souls, 1842—Riddle (J. E.) Scripture History, 1859—
    Leighton (Abp. R.) Commentary on St. Peter, 2 vol.
    portrait; and others (17)
20 Hughes (H.) Female Characters of Holy Writ, 3 vol.
    1845-7 — Duncan (H.) Sacred Philosophy of the Sea-
    sons, 4 vol. *plates, Edinb.* 1838—Female Revolutionary
    Plutarch, 3 vol. *portraits, half calf,* 1806 (12)
21 Chambers (T. K.) Manual of Diet in Health and Disease,
    1875; &c. (4)
22 Cumberland (R.) The Observer, 3 vol. *half calf,* 1817—
    Taylor (W. C.) Modern British Plutarch, 1846; &c. (9)
23 Gray (J. C.) Biblical Museum, 5 vol. *half morocco* 1871-3
24 Stowe (H. B.) Uncle Tom's Cabin, 27 *illustrations by G.*
    Cruikshank, 1852—Key to Uncle Tom's Cabin, *portrait,*
    1853 (2)
25 Lathbury (T.) Convocation of the Church of England, 1843
    —Birks (T. R.) Bible and Modern Thought — Way-
    land (F.) Elements of Moral Science—The Churchman
    Armed, by eight Clergymen, 1864; and others (21)
26 School Books various (63)

27 Harmony of the Gospels, 1836—M'Neile (H.) Church and
the Churches, 1847—Flavel (J.) Method of Grace—
Hanna (W.) Last Day of our Lord's Passion, *Edinb.*
1864; and others   (28)
28 Moseley (H.) Mechanics applied to the Arts, 1839—Adam
(A.) Roman Antiquities, 100 *illustrations*, 1835; and
others   (34)
29 Elegant Extracts, Prose, Verse, Epistles, 18 vol. *vignettes,
smooth red morocco, g. e.*   *Sharpe,* 1810
30 Irving (D.) Elements of Composition, *calf*, 1821; and
others   (25)
31 Tytler (A. F.) Universal History, 6 vol. 1839 — Keightley
(T.) History of England, 2 vol. 1845; &c.   (20)
32 Hodge (C.) Commentary on the Romans—Brown (D.) on
the same, *Glasgow*, 1860—Prime (S. I.) Power of
Prayer, 1860; &c.   (45)
33 Key (T. H.) Latin Grammar, 1846—Robson (J.) Con-
structive Latin Exercises, 1850; and other School
Books, &c.   (77)
34 Bibles, Common Prayers, Hymn Books, &c.   (41)
35 Combe (A.) Principles of Physiology, *Edinb.* 1834—Withering (W.) British Botany, *plates*, 1845—Conversations on Botany, *coloured plates*, 1840; &c.   (22)
36 Owen (J.) Select Works, 3 vol. 1831—Sermons or Homilies, 2 vol. 1820; and others   (22)
37 Ryle (J. C.) Expository Thoughts on the Gospels: S.
Matthew, 1856—Mark, 1859—Luke, 2 vol. 1858 —
John, 3 vol. 1865   (7)
38 Kitto (J.) Daily Bible Illustrations, Morning and Evening
series, 8 vol. *illustrated*   1850-4
39 Milner (J.) and T. Haweis, History of the Church, 4 vol.
1847—Chalmers (T.) Sabbath Scripture Readings, 2 vol.
1852—Daily Scripture Readings, 2 vol. 1853   (8)
40 Ryle (J. C.) Home Truths, 7 vol. 1860—Law (H.) "Christ
is All," 4 vol. 1857-8—Blunt (H.) Works, 7 vol. 1836-
45   (18)
41 Evans (R. W.) Scripture Biography, 2 vol. *fronts.* 1834-5—
Brock (W.) Biographical Sketch of Sir H. Havelock,
portrait, 1858; &c.   (15)
42 Wordsworth (C.) Greece, Pictorial, Descriptive and Historical, *nearly* 400 *steel and wood engravings, after C.
Fielding, D. Cox and other Artists, morocco gilt, g. e.* 1840
43 Bartlett (W. H.) Footsteps of our Lord and his Apostles,
engravings   1852
44 Howe (J.) Works, with Memoir by E. Calamy, *port.* 1844
45 Hall (R.) Works, by O. Gregory, 6 vol. LARGE PAPER,
portrait   1832

46 Quicherat (L.) Thesaurus Poeticus Linguæ Latinæ
  Paris, 1859
47 Browne (E. H.) Exposition of the XXXIX Articles 1864
48 Macaulay (Lord) Critical and Historical Essays, *port.* 1850
49 Doddridge (P.) Family Expositor, *portrait*   1827
50 Cambridge Prize Poems, 2 vol. *Camb.* 1817 — Lowth (Bp.
  R.) Sacred Poetry of the Hebrews, 1847—Herbert (G.)
  Poems, *portrait;* and others   (13)
51 Bickersteth (E. H.) Condensed Notes on Scripture, 1854—
  Echoes of Apostolic Teaching—Birks (T. R.) Memoir of
  the Rev. E. Bickersteth, 2 vol. *portrait,* 1853; &c. (7)
52 Horne (T. H.) Introduction to the Scriptures, 4 vol. *facsimiles, half calf gilt*   1823
53 Bible (Pictorial) 3 vol. *many hundred woodcuts,* 1836—Pictorial Edition of the Book of Common Prayer, with
  Notes by H. Stebbing, *woodcut illustrations, n. d. ;
  together* 4 vol. *calf gilt*   *C. Knight*
54 Bible (Holy) with Commentary, &c. by Adam Clarke, 6 vol.
  portrait, calf, m. e.   1840
55 Bible (Holy) with Commentary by C. Girdlestone, 6 vol.
                            1842
56 Dalton (W.) Commentary on the New Testament, 2 vol.
  1842—Gurnall (W.) Christian in Complete Armour,
  1837—Cecil (R.) Original Thoughts on Scripture, *portrait,* 1848; &c.   (5)
57 Alford (H.) Greek Testament, 4 vol. in 5   1854-61
58 Tait (W.) Exposition of the Hebrews, 2 vol.   1845
59 Foxe (J.) Acts and Monuments, by G. Townsend, 8 vol.
  portrait and plates   1843-9
60 Huntingdon (Selina, Countess of) Life and Times, 2 vol.
  portrait, 1840—Evans (J. H.) Memoir and Remains,
  portrait, 1852—Sidney (E.) Life of Rowland Hill, *portrait,* 1835; and others   (7)
61 Light in the Dwelling, 1846 — Gold and the Gospel,
  1853   (2)
62 Skelton (P.) Complete Works, by R. Lynam, 6 vol. 1824
63 Stier (R.) Words of the Lord Jesus, by W. B. Pope, 8 vol.
                        Edinb. 1855-8
64 Baxter (R.) Practical Works, by W. Orme, 23 vol. *portrait*
                            1830
65 Wesley (J.) Works, 14 vol. *portrait,* 1829 — Explanatory
  Notes upon the New Testament, 2 vol. 1831   (16)
66 Watson (R.) Works, with Life by T. Jackson, 12 vol. *portrait*   1834
67 Mitford (W.) History of Greece, with Memoir, &c. by
  Lord Redesdale, 8 vol.   1829
68 Cruden (A.) Concordance, *portrait, half calf*   1825

69 Robinson (T.) Scripture Characters, 4 vol. 1811—Daubeney
(C.) Discourses, 3 vol. 1821—Macknight (J.) Translation of the Epistles, 4 vol. *Edinb.* 1820 ; &c. (13)

70 Home Friend, 4 vol. *illustrated*, 1852-4;—Pastor's Assistant, vol. I to III, in 1 vol.; &c. (17)

71 Simeon (C.) Entire Works, by T. H. Horne, 21 vol. 1832-3

72 Hook (N.) Roman History, 6 vol. *maps*, 1823—Russell's
History of Modern Europe, 6 vol. 1827 (12)

73 Ellicott (C. J.) Commentaries, Pastoral Epistles, 1856—
Philippians, &c. 1857—Galatians, 1854—Ephesians,
1855 (4)

74 Sunday at Home, for 1861, 3, 4, 7, 8, *illustrated* 5 *vol.*

75 Good Words, for 1862, 3, 4, 5, 8, 9, 71, *illustrated, half
calf* 7 *vol.*

76 Dickens (C.) Household Words, vol. I to III, *half calf*,
1850-51—Sunday Magazine, for 1865; and others, 9 *vol.*

77 Parker Society, complete set, *with the exception of No.* 1,
2, 3, 4, 15, *viz.* Ridley's Works, Sandy's Sermons, Pilk-
ington's Works, Hutchinson's Works, M. Coverdale's
Writings, 1842, &c. 50 *vol.*

78 Eadie (J.) Commentary on the Ephesians, 1854—Walker
(S.) Lectures on the Church Catechism, 1836—Pratt
(J. H.) Eclectic Notes, 1856—Salter (H. G.) Book of
Illustrations, 1840 ; &c. (5)

79 Montgomery (J.) Poetical Works, *portrait*, 1850—Young
(E.) Night Thoughts, by G. Gilfillan, *Edinb.* 1853 (2)

80 Buxton (Sir T. F.) Memoirs, *portrait and cuts*, 1851—
Forster (C.) Correspondence between Bp. J. Jebb and
A. Knox, 2 vol. 1834—Martyn (H.) Journals and Let-
ters, by Bp. S. Wilberforce, 2 vol. *port.* 1837 ; &c. (7)

81 Barnes (A.) Notes on the New Testament, 6 vol. in 3, *half
calf*, 1846—On Isaiah, 3 vol. 1847—Daniel, 2 vol. in 1,
1853—Revelation, 1852, Editions edited by Dr. J. Cumming, *maps and cuts ;* and others (11)

82 Cumming (J.) Scripture Readings, Genesis, 1853—S. Matthew to S. John, 4 vol. 1853 ; &c. (6)

83 Bradley (C.) Practical Sermons, 2 vol. 1843—Johnson (J.)
Sermons, 2 vol. 1850—Vaughan (H.) Nine Sermons,
1837—Scholefield (J.) Sermon Notes, 1856 ; &c. (9)

84 Ecce Homo, 1866—King (Lord Chancellor) Primitive
Church, 1843—Overton (C.) Expository Preacher, 2 vol.
1850—Gregg (T. D.) Mystery of God Finished, 1861;
and others (9)

85 Roget (P. M.) Animal and Vegetable Physiology, 2 vol.
illustrated *Pickering*, 1834

86 Chronicle of Cranborne, in the County of Dorset, *frontispiece and map* 1841

87 Sumner (Bp. J. B.) Expositions on the Gospels, &c.
various (7)

88 Pearson (Bp. J.) Exposition of the Creed, 2 vol. *portrait,*
Oxford, 1820—Jay (W.) Morning Exercises, 2 vol. 1839
—Jebb (Bp. J.) Practical Theology, 2 vol. 1830—Camp-
bell (G.) Four Gospels, 3 vol. *Edinb.* 1812 ; &c.   (11)

89 Bather (E.) Sermons, 2 vol. *half calf,* 1829—Paley (W.)
Natural Theology, 1810—Arnold (T.) Sermons, 1829 ;
&c.   (10)

90 Le Bas (C. W.) Sermons, 2 vol. 1828—Wilson (D.) Ser-
mons, 1818—Leighton (R.) Eighteen Sermons, 1745—
Sherlock (Bp. T.) Discourses preached at the Temple
Church, 1824 ; &c.   (11)

91 Loudon (J. C.) Encyclopædia of Cottage, Farm and Villa
Architecture and Furniture, *over* 2000 *illustrations,* 1833
—Floricultural Cabinet, 3 vol. in 1, *coloured plates,* 1833-
35 ; &c.   (4)

92 Hutton (C.) Recreations in Mathematics, &c. by E. Riddle,
1840—Cresswell (D.) Maxima and Minima, *Camb.* 1817 ;
and others   (8)

93 Brande (W. T.) Manual of Chemistry, 3 vol. *illustrated,*
1821—Hall (M.) Diseases of Females, *plates ;* &c. (10)

94 Mosheim (J. L.) Ecclesiastical History, 2 vol. *frontispiece,*
Glasgow, 1829 — Robinson (J.) Archæologia Græca,
1807—Taylor (W. C.) Students' Manual of Modern History, 1851—Wood (T.) Mosaic Creation, 1811; &c. (10)

95 Novum Testamentum Græcum, English Notes by E. Valpy,
3 vol. 1826—Schleusneri (J. F.) Novum Lexicon Græco-
Latinum in Novum Test. 2 vol. *Lipsiæ,* 1808 ; &c. (7)

96 Dammii Lexicon Homericum, 2 vol. *Glasguæ,* 1833—
Brasse (J.) Greek Gradus, 1828 ; &c.   (5)

97 Walker's Pronouncing Dictionary, by B. H. Smart, 1836—
Crabb (G.) English Synonymes, 1824 ; &c.   (4)

98 Butler (Bp. J.) Works, by Bp. S. Halifax, 2 vol. *portrait,*
Edinb. 1816—Newton (J.) Works, *portrait, ib.* 1828—
Locke (J.) Common-Place-Book to the Bible, *portraits,*
1824 ; &c.   (7)

99 Macknight (J.) Harmony of the Four Gospels, 2 vol. 1819
—Milner (I.) Sermons, 2 vol. 1820—Isherwood (J.)
Three Dissertations, *Oxford,* 1835 ; &c.   (14)

100 Juvenalis Satiræ XVI, a G. A. Ruperti, 2 vol. *frontispiece,*
russia, Lipsiæ, 1801—Cæsaris Commentarii, F. Oudendorpii, 1825; and others   (23)

101 Oliver (S.) Grammar of the Inglish Language, 1825—
Guthrie (W.) Grammar of Geography, *maps,* 1819 ; and
others   (24)

102 White (H. K.) Remains, by R. Southey, 2 vol. *port.* 1816
—Alison (A.) Essays on Taste, 2 vol. *Edinb.* 1811—
Stewart (J.) Outlines of Discourses, *ib.* 1860 ; &c. (8)

103 Nichols (W. A.) National Drawing Master, *plates, Acker-mann*—Oriental Annual, *engravings*, 1834 ; &c.   (4)
104 Reid (T.) Inquiry into the Human Mind, *Glasgow*, 1817—Mill (J.) Elements of Political Economy, 1821 ; &c. (13)
105 Paley (W.) Evidences of Christianity, 2 vol. 1817—Middleton (C.) Life of Cicero, 2 vol. *portrait*, 1824—Jortin (J.) Sermons, 4 vol. 1771 ; &c.   (16)
106 Hume (D.) History of England, vol. I to VI, 1818 ; and others, *odd*   (19)
107 Macgillivray (W.) Rapacious Birds of Great Britain, *cuts*, 1836 ; &c.   (12)
108 Blunt (J.) Reformation in England, 1832 ; &c.   (50)
109 Original Family Sermons, vol. I to IV, 1833—Dallas (A.) Cottager's Guide to the New Testament, 6 vol. 1845-7 ; &c.   (15)
110 Hughes (T. S.) Divines of the Church of England, *various volumes*   (12)
111 Commentary upon the Bible, from Henry and Scott, 6 vol. 1836-8—Townsend (G.) Pentateuch, &c. chronologically arranged, 2 vol. 1845 ; &c.   (9)
112 Philidor (A. D.) Studies of Chess, 2 vol. *diagrams*, 1814—Smith (E.) Foods, *illustrated*, 1874—Farrar (F. W.) Eric, *Edinb.* 1859 ; &c.   (10)
113 Leland (J.) Deistical Writers, 2 vol. 1766—Divine Authority, 2 vol. 1739—Mant (R.) Sermons, 3 vol. *Oxford*, 1815 ; &c.   (11)
114 Homer's Iliad, by I. C. Wright, Books I-XII, *Camb.* 1861 ; &c.   (17)
115 Bible (Holy) *Oxford*, 1836—Hymns, Ancient and Modern, with Tunes ; &c.   (7)
116 Conybeare (J.) Defence of Reveal'd Religion, 1732 ; and others, *mostly odd*   (17)
117 Noel (M. M.) Leçons Françaises de Littérature, *calf, Bruxelles*, 1836—Voyages en France et Autres Pays, 5 vol. *portraits and plates, Paris*, 1818 ; &c.   (15)
118 Goulburn (E. M.) Idle World, 1855—Close (F.) Church Architecture, 1844—How (W. W.) Plain Words, *second and third series* ; &c.   (18)
119 Crockford's Clerical Directory, 1876—Clergy List, 1876 ; &c.   (6)
120 Duportus (J.) Musæ Subsecivæ, *Cantab.* 1676 ; &c.   (13)
121 Horace, Œuvres Complètes, par P. Daru, 4 vol. *Paris*, 1819 ; &c.   (17)
122 Cobbett (W.) English Gardener, 1829—Jemmat (W.) Abridgment of Dr. Preston's Works, 1648 ; &c.   (25)
123 Murray's Hand-book for Shropshire, Cheshire and Lancashire, *map*, 1870 ; &c.   (10)
124 Napoleon's Book of Fate, by H. Kirchenhoffer, *frontispiece*, 1825 ; &c.   (39

QUARTO.

125 Bickersteth (E. H.) Yesterday, To-Day and for Ever, *printed within red borders* 1873
126 Harris (J.) Altar of the Household, *front.* *Cassell, n. d.*
127 Cumming (J.) Daily Family Devotion 1854
128 Johnson (S.) Dictionary of the English Language, by H. J. Todd, 3 vol. *portrait, calf* 1827
129 Moody (C.) The New Testament Expounded and Illustrated, 2 parts 1849-51
130 Family Prayer Book, edited by E. Garbett, &c. 1864— Book of Family Prayer, by Clergymen of the Church of England, 1844—Holy Bible, *with marginal references*, 1840 (3)
131 Commentary, wholly Biblical, 3 vol. *maps, morocco, g. e.* *Bagster,*
132 Bible (Holy) by D'Oyly and Mant, 3 vol. *maps and engravings, calf,* Camb. 1823—Book of Common Prayer, with Notes by R. Mant, *calf, Oxford,* 1822 (4)
133 Henry (M.) Exposition of the Old and New Testament, by G. Burder and J. Hughes, 6 vol.—Miscellaneous Writings, together 7 vol. *maps and plates, calf, binding of two vol. broken* 1806-11
134 Baxter (R.) Saints Everlasting Rest, *front. by Cross,* 1658
135 Thénot (P.) Cours Complet de Paysage, 60 *plates, Paris,* 1834—Clark (J.) Amateur's Assistant, *plates,* 1826; &c. (4)
136 Quin (E.) Historical Atlas, *coloured maps, half russia,* 1836; &c. (6)
137 Lives of the Primitive Fathers, 1732—Moore (D.) Daily Devotion, 1847; &c. (4)

FOLIO.

138 Picart (B.) Ceremonies and Religious Customs, 7 vol. in 6, *plates, calf, binding of one vol. broken* 1733-9
139 Oxford Chronological Tables of Ancient History, *half bound* *Oxford,* 1835
140 Scapulæ (J.) Lexicon Græco-Latinum, cum Indice, *calf* *Oxonii,* 1820
141 Maps of the Society for the Diffusion of Useful Knowledge, 2 vol. 218 *maps and index, half russia* 1844
142 Illustrated London News, from Jan. 1851 to Dec. 1853, and Jan. 1860 to June 1864, 11 vol. *half calf;* and one other (12)
143 Bates (W.) Works, *portrait by White* 1700
144 Babington (Bp. G.) Workes, *portrait by Elstrack,* 1622— Sanderson (Bp. R.) XXXV Sermons, *portrait by Dalle,* 1681; &c. (3)

145 Reynolds (E.) Works, *portrait by Loggan*, 1658—Usher
(Bp. J.) Body of Divinitie, *port. by Marshall*, 1653 (2)
146 Quick (J.) Synodicon in Gallia Reformata, 2 vol. *portrait
by Sturt, and frontispiece* 1692
147 Castelnau (M. de) Reigns of Francis II and Charles IX
of France, 1724; and one other (2)
148 Burkitt (W.) on the New Testament, *portrait* (*mounted*),
no title, half calf
149 Day of Rest for 1873 and 5; and others (4)
150 Keach (B.) Tropologia, or, a Key to Open Scripture
Metaphors, in 2 vol. *half calf* 1671-2
151 Penny Magazine, vol. I, II, III, *woodcuts*, 1832-4—Plans
of the Stars, 6 *large plates*, 1836 (6)

OTHER PROPERTIES.

OCTAVO ET INFRA.

LOT
153 Speke (J. H.) Journal of the Discovery of the Source of
the Nile, *map and numerous illustrations* 1863
154 Newton (C. T.) Discoveries in Halicarnassus, Cnidus and
Branchidæ, *text 2 vol. with plates and cuts, and series of
97 large lithographic plates, in folio,* 1862 (3)
155 Forbes (J. D.) Travels through the Alps, *plates and cuts*
Edinb. 1843
156 Macgillivray (W.) Natural History of Dee Side and
Bræmar, *maps and illustrations, presentation copy from
Prince Albert* *privately printed,* 1855
157 Gladstone (W. E.) Homer and the Homeric Age, 3 vol.
uncut, maps *Oxford,* 1858
158 Campbell (J. Lord) Lives of the Lord Chancellors, 7 vol.
1846-7
159 Josephus (Flavius) Works, by W. Whiston, 2 vol. *plates,
calf gilt, m. e.* 1852
160 Tillotson (Arbp. J.) Works, by T. Birch, 10 vol. *portrait,
calf* 1820
161 Scrope (G. P.) Volcanos, *map and illustrations* 1862
162 Borrow (G.) Bible in Spain, 3 vol. *half calf* 1843
163 Hamilton (W. J.) Researches in Asia Minor, &c. 2 vol.
plates 1842
164 Burke (E.) Speeches, 4 vol. 1816
165 Smith (A.) Wealth of Nations, by J. R. McCulloch,
portraits *Edinb.* 1850

166 D'Aubigné (J. H. M.) Reformation in Germany, 4 vol. 1841
167 D'Aubigné (J. H. M.) Germany, England and Scotland
1848
168 Mitford (W.) History of Greece, 10 vol. *calf* 1814
169 Hume (D.) and T. Smollett, History of England, 13 vol.
portraits of the authors 1825
170 Mure (W.) Language and Literature of Antient Greece,
3 vol. 1850
171 Wilkinson (J. G.) Topography of Thebes, *plates* 1835
172 Bible (Holy) with Commentary from Henry and Scott,
6 vol. 1838
173 Reformation and Anti-Reformation in Germany, 2 vol. in 1,
1845—Classical Studies by B. Sears, B. B. Edwards, &c.
Boston, 1843; &c. (3)
174 Howse (J.) Grammar of the Cree Language, 1844—Forbes
(D.) Hindústání Grammar, 1862 (2)
175 Rollin (M.) Ancient History, 6 vol. *portrait* 1839
176 Sharpe (S.) History of Egypt, 2 vol. 1852
177 Brooke (J.) Borneo and Celebes, 2 vol. *plates, maps, &c.*
1848—Denham and Clapperton's Travels in Africa,
2 vol. *plates*, 1828—Fraser (J. B.) Journey from Constantinople to Tehran, 2 vol. *fronts.* 1838; &c. (7)
178 Hughes (T. S.) Travels in Greece and Albania, 2 vol.
plates, 1830—Laborde (M. L. de) Mount Sinai and
Petra, *illustrated*, 1836; and others (7)
179 Harcourt (J. V.) Doctrine of the Deluge, 2 vol. 1838—
McNeile (H.) Lectures on the Church of England, 1840
—Moore (G.) Use of the Body in relation to the Mind,
1847 (4)
180 Proceedings of the Zoological Society of England, 1851 to
1858 (*wanting* 1855), *coloured plates* (7)
181 Proceedings of the Royal Geographical Society, vol. 1,
1855, to vol. 7, 1863, *maps*, 7 vol. *half calf*; &c. (11)
182 Proceedings of the Geological Society, vol. 1, 1834, No. 31,
73 to 77, 80, 1, 4, 5, 7, 9, 90 (1852-67)—Transactions
of the Geological Society, vol. 3 part 3 (1835), vol. 7
part 2 and 3, 1845-6—Plates and Maps to the same, for
vol. 1, 2, 3—Ormerod (G. W.) Index to the Transactions,
&c. 1858—Catalogue of the Library, with Supplement,
2 vol. 1846; &c. *8vo. and 4to.* (24)
183 Proceedings of the Royal Society, No. 19, 58, 9, 60, 65 to
81, *plates*, 21 Nos.—Journal of the United Service
Institution, No. 43 to 62, with Appendix to vol. 11, 12,
13, 14, 1867-71, 23 Nos.; &c. (47)
184 Clarac (F. De) Musée de Sculpture Antique et Moderne,
vol. 1, 2, and 3, part 1, in 4 vol. *half calf, Paris*, 1841;
part 14 and 15, 1849-50 (6)
185 Gems, Collection of 61 Casts, after Canova, in 2 boxes

186 Chenu (J. C.) Manuel de Conchyliogie, 2 vol. in 3 parts,
numerous illustrations, many coloured   *Paris*, 1859-62
187 Beche (H. T. De La) Geological Observer, *illustrated* 1853
188 Menke (K. T.) Malakozoologische Blätter, 10 vol. in 6,
plates, half calf   *Cassel*, 1853-62
189 Pfeiffer (L.) Monographia Heliceorum Viventium, 4 vol.
Lipsiæ, 1848
190 Herschel (Sir J. F. W.) Admiralty Manual of Scientific
Enquiry, *maps, &c.* 1851—Another edition, 1849   (2)
191 Herschel (Sir J. F. W.) Admiralty Manual of Scientific
Enquiry, *maps, &c.* 1851   *2 copies*
192 Plinii Historia Naturalis, cum Notis J. Harduini, 10 vol.
Lipsiæ, 1778, *&c.*
193 Brown (T.) Land and Fresh Water Conchology, 27 *plates*,
1845—Reeve (L.) Land and Fresh Water Mollusks,
illustrated, 1863; &c.   (5)
194 Hunt (R.) Poetry of Science, 1848—Plurality of Worlds,
front. 1853—Miller (H.) Testimony of the Rocks, *cuts*,
Edinb. 1857—First Impressions, 1847—Jackson (J. R.)
What to Observe, 1841—Poole (R. S.) Genesis of the
Earth and of Man, 1860   (6)
195 Clarke (E. D.) Syllabus of Lectures in Mineralogy, *Camb.*
1807— Greek Marbles, *plates, ib.* 1809, in 1 vol.—
Morris (J.) Catalogue of British Fossils, *interleaved*,
1843—Nicol (J.) Manual of Mineralogy, *Edinb.* 1849;
and others   (6)
196 Lea (J.) Contributions to Geology, *tinted plates, Philadelphia*, 1833—The Geologist, *illustrated*, 1858—Forbes
(E.) Tertiary Fluvio-Marine Formation of the Isle of
Wight, *plates*, 1856—Lycett (J.) The Cotteswold Hills,
1857; and others   (9)
197 Adams (C. B.) Catalogue of Shells Collected at Panama,
New York, 1852—Macfayden (J.) Flora of Jamaica,
1837 — Daubeney (C.) Active and Extinct Volcanos,
map, &c. 1826—Bell (T.) History of British Reptiles,
cuts, 1839; &c.   (6)
198 Wollaston (T. V.) Coleopterous Insects of Madeira in the
British Museum, 1857—Steenstrup (J. J.) Alteration
of Generations, *plates*, 1845—Hopkins (E.) Connexion
of Geology with Terrestrial Magnetism, 24 *plates*, 1844;
and others   (7)
199 Luden (H.) Geschichte des Teutschen Volkes, 10 vol.
Gotha, 1825-35
200 Meyer (J.) Physik der Schweiz, *Leipzig*, 1854—Bronn
(H. G.) Entwickelungs-Gesetze der organischen Welt,
Stuttgart, 1858—Cotta (B.) Geologische Bilder, *illustrated, Leipzig*, 1854 — Bronn (H. G.) Allgemeine
Zoologie, *Stuttgart*, 1850; and others, *German*   (20)

201 De Santarem (Vicomte) Cosmographie et de la Carto-
graphie, 2 vol. *Paris*, 1849 — Délandre (M. C.) Le
Morbihan, *Vannes*, 1847—Barrande (J.) Défense des
Colomis, part 3, 1865—Payrandeau (B. C.) Catalogue
des Annelides et des Mollusques de l'ile de Corré, *plates*,
Paris, 1826 ; and others, French   (21)
202 Eichhoff (F. W.) Vergleichung der Sprachen von Europa
und Indien, *Leipzig*, 1840 ; and others   (21)
203 Hausman (J. F. L.) Handbuch der Mineralogie, 3 vol.
interleaved, *Gottingen*, 1813 — Krug (W. T.) Theo-
retischen Philosophie, &c. 4 vol. *Königsberg*, 1819, &c.
—Jakop (L. H. von) Die Staatsfinanzwissenschaft, 2 vol.
Halle, 1821—Kant (J.) Critik der reinen Vernunst,
2 vol. *Leipzig*, 1818 — Luden (H.) Geschichte der
Teutschen, 3 vol. *Jena*, 1842 ; and others   (25)
204 Zeitschift der Deutschen Geologischen Gesellschaft, 27
various parts, *plates*, *Berlin*, 1853-66—Jahrbücher des
Vereins für Naturkunde im Herzogthum Nassau,
plates, some coloured, 17 parts, various, *Wiesbaden*,
1845-63
205 Burmeister (H.) Geschichte der Schöpfung, *illustrated*,
Leipzig, 1851—Montagna (C.) Intorno all'esistenza di
Resti Organizzati, *plates, morocco, Torino*, 1866 —
D'Halloy (J. J. D.) Abrégé de Géologie, *illustrated*,
Bruxelles, 1862—Roth (J.) Der Vesuv und die Umge-
bung von Neapel, *plates, Berlin*, 1857 ; &c.   (6)
206 Rossmässler (E. A.) Iconographie der Land-und Süss-
wasser-Mollusken Europa's, vol. 3, 6 parts in 3, *highly
coloured plates, Leipzig*, 1854—Stabile (J.) Mollusques
Terrestres Vivants du Piémont, *coloured plates, Milan*,
1864 ; and others   (7)
207 Hüllman (K. D.) Stœdtewesen des Mittelalters, 4 vol.
half calf, Bonn, 1826—Mousson (A.) Mollusken von
Java, *coloured plates ;* and others   (11)
208 Wachler (L.) Handbuch der Geschichte der Litteratur,
4 vol. in 2, *half calf, Leipzig*, 1833—Ukert (F. A.)
Geographie der Griechen und Römer, 2 vol. in 3, *Weimar*,
1816 — Bæhr (J. C. F.) Geschichte der Römischen
Literatur, *Carlsruhe*, 1832 ; &c.   (8)
209 Vermiglioli (G. B.) Lezioni Elementari di Archeologia,
2 vol. in 1, *Milano*, 1824—Hempel (A. F.) Anfangs-
gründe der Anatomie, 2 vol. *Göttingen*, 1823 ; &c.   (9)
210 Quicherat (L.) et A. Daveluy, Dictionnaire Latin-Français
Paris, 1858
211 Bacon-Tacon (J. J.) Recherches sur les Origines Celtiques,
2 vol. *portrait, uncut*   *Paris, An VI*
212 Ciceronis Opera, ex recensione J. A. Ernesti, 8 vol. in 9,
half calf   *Halæ*, 1820

213 Rocher (G. du) Histoire des Temps Fabuleux, 4 vol. *half calf, Paris,* 1824—Rüppell (E.) Reise in Abyssinien, 2 vol. *Frankfurt,* 1838—Say (J. B.) Traité d'Économie Politique, 2 vol. *Paris,* 1819; and others (13)

214 D'Ossat (Cardinal) Letres, avec des Notes de A. de la Houssaie, 5 vol. *Amsterdam,* 1714; and others (17)

215 Ritter (H.) Histoire de la Philosophie, par C. J. Tissot, 3 vol. *Paris,* 1836—Humboldt (A. de) Essai Politique de la Nouvelle-Espagne, 5 vol. *ib.* 1811—Malle (M. Dureau de la) Recherches sur la Topographie de Carthage, *plans, ib.* 1835; &c. (10)

216 Heeren (A. H. L.) Historische Werke, Ideen, 2 vol. in 5; Europäische Staatensystems, 2 vol. *Göttingen,* 1822-6 —Müller (K. O.) Geschichten Hellenischer Stämme, 3 vol. 1820; &c. (11)

217 Pittakys (K. S.) l'Ancienne Athènes, *Athènes,* 1835— Volney (C. F. C.) Les Ruines, *front. Paris,* 1808; and others (21)

218 Denina (C.) Rivoluzioni d'Italia, 6 vol. *portrait, Venezia,* 1816; and others (10)

219 Tennemann (W. G.) Geschichte der Philosophie, *Leipzig,* 1829—Spittler's Europäischen Staaten, 2 vol. *Berlin,* 1823; and others (25)

220 Sophoclis Tragœdiæ Septem, Gr. cum Annotatione Brunckii, &c. 3 vol. *Oxonii,* 1820—Homeri Odyssea, cum Scholiis Veteribus, 2 vol. *ib.* 1827—Herodoti Historiæ, edidit T. Gaisford, *ib.* 1830—Æschyli Tragœdiæ, G. Commentario C. G. Schütz, 5 vol. *Halæ,* 1809; and others (19)

221 Terentii Comœdiæ, cum Notis Variorum, 2 vol. *Lugd. Bat.* 1686—Thucydides de Bello Peloponnesiaco, 2 vol. *Lips.* 1820—Maps and Plans to Thucydides—Maps to Herodotus, 1825; and other Greek and Latin Classics (29)

222 Robertson (W.) Works, by R. Lynam, 6 vol. *portraits and maps* 1826

223 Pantalogia (The), by J. M. Good, &c. 12 vol. *coloured and other plates, imperfect, with all faults* 1813

224 Cornhill Magazine, *illustrated, various numbers,* 1860-75 (93)

225 Stanley (A. P.) Sermons and Essays on the Apostolical Age *Oxford,* 1847

226 Turner (S.) Sacred History of the World, 3 vol. 1833— Crombie (A.) Natural Theology, 2 vol. 1829; and others

227 Butler (Bp. S.) Works, 2 vol. *calf, Oxford,* 1836—Sumner (J. B.) Records of the Creation, 2 vol. *calf,* 1818; and others (10)

228 Drummond (W.) Origines, 4 vol. 1824

229 Aikin (J.) Annals of the Reign of George III, 2 vol.
    1820; and others   (15)
230 Todhunter (I.) Conic Sections, *Camb.* 1858; &c.   (6)
231 Aldrich (H.) Elements of Civil Architecture, *plates*
                                   Oxonii, 1789
232 Kames' Elements of Criticism, 2 vol. *Edinb.* 1817 —
    Whately (R.) Elements of Logic, 1831; &c.   (7)
233 Mackintosh (Sir J.) History of England, vol. I to VIII,
    1830—Dunham (S. A.) History of the Germanic Em-
    pire, 3 vol. 1834; and others   (17)
234 School Books, various   (37)
235 Bonar (H.) Prophetical Landmarks, 1847—Taylor (I.)
    Saturday Evening, 1842; and others   (25)
236 Porti (M. A.) Dictionarium Ionicum, Gr. et Lat. *Oxonii,*
    1821—Constantini (R.) Lexicon Græcola, 1568; &c.(6)
237 Lodge (E.) Peerage, 1860; and others   (7)
238 Edinburgh and Quarterly Review, various Nos.; &c.
                                  a parcel
239 Mantell (G.) Geology of the South East of England,
    illustrated, 1833—Ingen-Housz (J.) Experiments upon
    Vegetables, 1779; and others   (16)
240 Robertson (W.) Works, by R. Lynan, 6 vol. *portraits, &c.*
    1826—Rennell (J.) Geography of Western Asia, 2 vol.
    1831—Geographical System of Herodotus, 2 vol. *maps,*
    1830; &c.   (11)
241 Mavor (W.) British Tourist, and Voyages and Travels,
    19 vol. odd; and others   (32)
242 Tylor (E. B.) Anahuac, *map and plates,* 1861—Arundell
    (V. J.) Seven Churches of Asia, *map,* 1828; &c. (9)
243 Trotter (A.) Finances of the North American Coast,
    map, 1839—Young (T.) Discoveries in Hieroglyphical
    Literature, 1823—Hamilton (W. G.) Parliamentary
    Logick, *portrait,* 1808; and others   (11)
244 Gilly (W. S.) Vigilantius and his Times, 1844—Carlyle
    (T.) Past and Present, 1843; &c.   (12)
245 Surtees (T.) Handley Cross, 5 Nos.—Choice Notes (His-
    tory), 1858; and others   (25)
246 Warr (D.) Lectures on the Pilgrim's Progress, 1832;
    and others   (23)
247 Dioscoridis Opera, Gr. et Lat. *russia, g. e. Parisiis,* 1549
    —Frontini (S. J.) Strategemata, &c. *old red morocco,*
    g. e. Amstelodami, 1661 — Dawes (R.) Miscellanea
    Critica, cum Notis T. Kidd, *Cantab.* 1817; &c.   (4)
248 Xenophon's Analysis, Gr. by J. F. Macmichael, 1852;
    and others   (18)
249 Hamilton (W. J.) Manual of Geography, 1859, 20 *copies;*
    and others   (58)
250 Senecæ Tragœdiæ, 1699; &c.   (5)

251 Pamphlets, &c. in 3 vol. &c.   (4)
252 MS. Remembrances for Order and Decency to be kept in
    the Upper House of Parliament, &c. *old red morocco
    gilt*
253 Speth (B.) Die Kunst in Italien, 3 vol. *plates, München,*
    1819 ; and others   (10)
254 Kock (Paul de) L'Enfant de ma Femme, *Paris,* 1842 ;
    and others   (25)
255 Kärcher (E.) Handwörterbuch der Lateinischen Sprache,
    Stuttgart, 1842 ; and others   (18)
256 Guizot (M.) Cours d'Histoire Moderne, *half morocco gilt*
                    Bruxelles, 1839
257 Molière, Œuvres Complètes, *portrait, half calf Paris,* 1843
258 Lamartine, Œuvres, *portrait and plates, calf gilt, m. e.*
                    Bruxelles, 1838
259 Spenser (E.) The Faerie Queen (Six books), *first edition
    of the whole work, russia, a portion of leaf* 325-6 *imper-
    fect*   *Lond. W. Ponsonbie,* 1596
260 Rollin (M.) Histoire Ancienne, 13 vol. in 14, *Paris,* 1769
    —Histoire Romaine, 16 vol. *ib.* 1803, *plates, bright old
    calf gilt*   (30)
261 Horatii Opera Omnia, with a Commentary by A. J. Mac-
    leane   1853
262 Novum Test. Græcum, English Notes by S. T. Bloomfield,
    2 vol. 1845—Novum Test. Gr. by E. Burton, 2 vol.
    Oxford, 1835   (4)
263 Bayle (P.) Dictionnaire Historique et Critique, augmenté
    de notes extraits de Chaufepié, Joly, Marchant, etc.
    16 vol. BEST EDITION, *calf gilt*   *Paris,* 1820
264 Mably (L'Abbé de) Collection Complète des Œuvres,
    15 vol. in 14, *calf*   *Paris,* 1794-95
265 Racine (J.) Œuvres, 5 vol. *calf gilt*   *Paris,* 1813
266 Molière, Œuvres, par M. Petitot, 6 vol. *portrait, calf gilt*
                    ib. 1812
267 Montesquieu (M. de) Œuvres Complettes, 6 vol. *portrait
    and map, calf gilt*   *ib.* 1816
268 Corneille (P.) Chefs-de-Œuvre, 3 vol. *calf gilt*   *ib.* 1814
269 Voltaire (M. de) Chefs-d'Œuvre Dramatiques, 4 vol.
    —Siècle de Louis XIV, 2 vol.—Precis du Siècle de
    Louis XV, *calf gilt, Paris,* 1808-10   (7)
270 Stael (Mad. de) Considerations sur la Révolution Fran-
    çaise, 3 vol. *Liege,* 1818—Lamartine (M. A. de) Voyage
    en Orient, 4 vol. *portrait, Paris,* 1835 ; &c.
271 Lamartine (A. de) Histoire de la Turquie, 8 vol. *Par.* 1855
272 Robinson (E.) Greek and English Lexicon to the New
    Testament, by S. Bloomfield, 1839—Novum Test. Græ-
    cum, by W. Trollope, 1837   (2)

273 Sismondi (J. C. L. S. de) Littérature du Midi de l'Europe,
4 vol. *half calf, Paris,*1813— Segur (Comtede) Mémoires
ou Souvenirs et Anecdotes, 3 vol. *fronts. ib.* 1825   (7)

274 Campan (Madame) Mémoires sur la Vie Privée de Marie-
Antoinette, 3 vol. *Paris,* 1826—Beugnot (A.) Histoire
de la Destruction du Paganisme en Occident, 2 vol. *ib.*
1835—Mignet (F. A.) Histoire de la Révolution, 2 vol.
Bruxelles, 1835; &c.   (10)

275 Villemain (M.) Cours de Littérature Française, 7 vol.
Paris, 1829-38; &c.   (17)

276 Sue (E.) Le Juif Errant, 15 vol. (1 *wanting*), 1844—Cervantes (M. de) Don Quichotte, par M. Florian, 6 vol.
fronts. Paris, 1810—Le Sage, Histoire de Gil Blas,
3 vol. *ib.* 1824; and others   (36)

277 Cæsar de Bello Gallico, by G. Long, 1853—Xenophon
Anabasis, by J. F. Macmichael, *map,* 1847—Xenophon
Anabasis, by C. Anthon, 1852; and others, Anthon's
Classics, &c.   (10)

278 Æschylus, Agamemnon, by T. W. Peile, 1844—Lexicon
to Æschylus, by W. Linwood, 1847—Tragedies, translated by R. Potter, *Oxford,* 1812—Sophoclis Tragœdiæ,
Gr. ex editione R. F. P. Brunck, 2 vol. *Oxonii,* 1814—
Sophoclis Antigone, by J. W. Donaldson, 1848—Phi-
loctetes, and 6 others, by T. Mitchell, *Oxford,* 1844, *&c.*
—Ellendt's Lexicon to Sophocles, *ib.* 1841; &c. (18)

279 Ruperti (G. A.) Commentarius in Taciti Annales, 1825—
Turner (D. W.) Notes on Herodotus, *Oxford,* 1848—
Cary (H.) Lexicon to Herodotus, *ib.* 1843; &c.   (4)

280 Livii Historiæ, ex Recensione A. Drakenborchii, cum Notis
J. B. L. Crevierii, 4 vol. *Oxonii,* 1818; and others (21)

281 Juvenal and Persius, Satires, by C. W. Stocker, *calf,* 1839
—Lucian, Selections from, by J. Walker, *half russia,*
Glasgow, 1823; &c.   (10)

282 Lucani (M. A.) Pharsalia, cum Notis H. Grotii, et R.
Bentleii, *Glasguæ,* 1816; &c.   (4)

283 Horace, Satires and Epistles, by T. Keightley, 1848; and
others   (9)

284 Novum Test. Græcum—Greek Lexicon, by W. Greenfield,
Bagster, in 1 vol. &c.   (3)

285 Virgilii Opera, cura J. Hunter, vol. I, 1810—Keightley
(T.) Notes on Virgil, 1846, in 1 vol.; and others, *all*
bound in calf with tuck   (4)

286 Lucian, Works, by J. Dryden and others, 4 vol. *portrait*
by Faithorne, calf, 1711; &c.   (11)

287 Chateaubriand (F. A. de) Itinéraire de Paris a Jérusalem,
2 vol. *map, Paris,* 1812—Pascal (B.) Les Provinciales,
portrait, ib. 1829—Beckford (W.) Vathek, *front.* 1815;
&c.   (8)

288 Lucretius (T.) of the Nature of Things, 2 vol. *plates by Du Guernier and others, old calf gilt* 1743
289 Terence, Comedies de, Mad. Dacier, 2 vol. *several outline plates by Picart, calf, Amsterdam,* 1724—Taciti Opera, ex editione J. J. Oberlini, 3 vol. 1817 ; &c. (42)
290 Valpy (F. E. J.) Second Greek Delectus, 1837 ; and others, School Books, &c. (26)
291 Lever's Tom Burke of " Ours," *plates by H. K. Browne,* 2 vol. *half morocco gilt* *Dublin,* 1844
292 Trollope's Orley Farm, 2 vol. *plates by Millais, half calf gilt* 1862
293 Pardoe (Miss) The City of the Magyar, 3 vol. *portrait,* 1849—Marriott's Blackgown Papers, 2 vol. *portrait,* 1846
294 Lever (C.) The O'Donoghue : a Tale of Ireland, *plates by Phiz, half calf, Dublin,* 1849—Dickens American Notes, *front.* 1850—G. Cruikshank's Discovery concerning Ghosts, *cuts,* 1863
295 Lever (C.) Charles O'Malley, the Irish Dragoon, 2 vol. *plates by Phiz, half calf* *Dublin,* 1841
296 Bollaert's Wars of Succession of Portugal and Spain, 2 vol. *plates,* 1870—Evans' Sugar Planter's Manual, *half calf,* 1847—Baxter's Impressions of Central Europe, 1850 ; and 2 others (6)
297 Johnson's Lives of the Poets, 4 vol. *portrait, calf,* 1783—Tomline's Memoirs of William Pitt, 3 vol. *calf* 1821
298 Cope's Natural History, *cuts, n. d.*—Smith's Diary of a Huntsman, *cuts,* 1841 (2)
299 Lemon (Mark) Loved at Last, a Story, 3 vol. *presentation copy from the author to Horace Mayhew, with autograph in each vol.* 1864
300 Borrow (G.) Lavengro, 3 vol. *portrait* 1851
301 Haliburton's Historical and Statistical Account of Nova Scotia, 2 vol. *map and plates* *Halifax,* 1829
302 German Album Amicorum, containing some German Drawings, Portraits, Historical Autographs, &c. *original calf binding* *ob. 4to.* 1759, *&c.*
303 Philosophy in Sport, *cuts by G. Cruikshank,* 1846—White's Natural History of Selbourne, *cuts,* 1833—Jesse's Gleanings of Natural History, *cuts* 1843
304 Poetical Effusions, *with 56 engravings by G. Cruikshank,* 1836, *scarce*—Wit and Wisdom, or the World's Jest Book, *cuts by Cruikshank, &c. n. d.* (2)
305 Dickens (C.) The Mystery of Edwin Drood, complete in the original Parts, *plates* 1870
306 Egan (Pierce) Finish to the Adventures of Tom, Jerry and Logic's Life in London, *numerous coloured plates by R. Cruikshank, cloth gilt* *roy. 8vo. n. d.*
307 Spenser (E.) Works with Notes by Aikin, 5 vol. 1842

308 Peter Schlemihl from the German of Von Chamisso, translated by Bowring, *plates by G. Cruikshank* 1861
309 Pollok (R.) Course of Time, FIRST EDITION, 2 vol. in 1,
morocco, g. e. scarce 1827
310 Clapthorne's Dramatic Works, 2 vol. *uncut, Pearson,* 1874
311 Poetry of Various Glees, Songs, &c. as performed at the
Harmonists, *front. calf gilt,* 1798—Carlisle's Tragedies
and Poems, *morocco extra* 1801
312 Reade (J. E.) Poetical Works, 4 vol. 1857—Pope's
Poetical Works, 4 vol. *portrait and plates, calf gilt,* 1787
313 Radcliffe (Anne) Posthumous Works, 4 vol. 1833
314 Philosophy in Sport, 3 vol. *cuts by G. Cruikshank, half
calf* 1827
315 Punch's Pocket Book for 1869-70, 2 vol. *coloured fronts.
morocco*—Punch's Humorous Songster, *front. plate*—
London Comic Songster, *front. plate, n. d.* (4)
316 Hamerton's Isles of Loch Awe, *cuts,* 1859—Michelet's
Priests, Woman and Families, translated by Cocks,
1846—" Ecce Homo," 1868 (3)
317 Denman (J.) The Drama Vindicated, 1835—Fairburn's
Cabinet of Amusement, *coloured frontispiece, n. d.*—
Kemble (J. P.) Macbeth and Richard the Third, 1817
—Heinschadel's Ologies of the Cranion and Phren,
1834 (5)
318 Shelley's Memorials, edited by Lady Shelley, *front.* 1862
—Trelawney's Recollections of the last days of Shelley
and Byron, *portrait,* 1858
319 Shelley Papers by T. Medwin, 1833—Shelley's Poetical
Works, *portrait and vignette,* 1853
320 Flim Flams, or the Life and Errors of my Uncle and his
Friends, 3 vol. *humorous plates, half calf* 1806
321 Lacroix (Paul) Vie Militaire et Religieuse au Moyen Age,
*woodcuts and numerous plates in gold and colours, mo-
rocco gilt* *imp. 8vo. Paris,* 1873
322 Shaffner (Col. T. P.) History of the United States of
America, *plates and vignette title,* 5 *Div. complete, n. d.*
L. P. P. C.
323 Stafford's Pacata Hibernia: Ireland Appeased and Reduced,
2 vol. *portraits and plates, half calf* 1821
324 Racine Œuvres Completes, *portrait and numerous plates,
half morocco, g. e.* *imp. 8vo. Paris, n. d.*
325 Cervantes as a Novelist, 2 parts in 1 vol. *coloured front.* 1822
326 Rogers (C.) The Modern Scottish Minstrel, 6 vol. *portraits
and vignettes* *Edinb.* 1855
327 Polish Tales, 3 vol. 1833—Maberly (Mrs.) Fashion and its
Votaries, 3 vol. 1848—Hewlett's College Life, or the
Proctor's Note Book, 3 vol. 1843 (9)

328 Boccaccio's Decameron, or Ten Days' Entertainment,
   portrait, half calf 1820
329 Forster's Life of Dickens, vol. III, *portrait and plates,*
   1874—Macaulay's History of England (Lib. Ed.)
   vol. II, 1856—Brougham's George III, *portraits,* 1847
   —Napier's Memoirs of Viscount Dundee, *portraits,*
   Edinb. 1859
330 Knight's Popular History of England, vol. VII, *portraits,*
   Sangster, n. d.—Alison's Europe (Lib. Ed.) vol. III,
   IV, V, 1835—Morell's Tales of the Genii, vol. I, *plates,*
   calf, 1820 ; and others (9)
331 Johnston's Notes on North America, 2 vol. *maps,* 1851—
   Napier (Col.) Excursions along the Shores of the
   Mediterranean, 2 vol. *front.* 1842—Moschzisker's German Literature, 2 vol. 1850 (6)
332 Kohl (J. G.) Popular History of America, 2 vol. 1862—
   Hassaurck's Four Years among Spanish Americans,
   1868—Barrow's Tour round Ireland, *plates by Maclise,*
   1836—New England and her Institutions, 1835 (5)
333 Strickland (Agnes) Pilgrims of Walsingham, FIRST
   EDITION, 3 vol. 1835—Lever (C.) Diary and Notes of
   Horace Templeton, 2 vol. 1849—Warburton's Rollo and
   his Race : or Footsteps of the Normans, 2 vol. *port.* 1848
   (7)

QUARTO.

334 Dodsworth (W.) Historical Account of the Cathedral
   Church of Salisbury, *plates, calf* 1814
335 Strickland (H. E.) and A. G. Melville, The Dodo, Soli-
   taire, and other Extinct Birds, *coloured and other plates*
   1848
336 Carpenter (W. H.) Pictorial Notices : consisting of a
   Memoir of Sir A. Van Dyck, *portraits* 1844
337 Scott (T.) Commentary on the Holy Bible, 6 vol. *maps,* 1839
338 Raoul-Rochette (M.) Peintures Antiques Inédites, *plates*
   coloured by hand *Paris,* 1836
339 Bezzi (G. A.) Life of Giovanni Angelico da Fiesole, *plates*
   on india paper, by G. Scharf, half morocco, m. e.
   Arundel Society, 1850
340 Ruskin (J.) Giotto and his Works in Padua, *plates, half*
   calf *ib.* 1854
341 Combe (T.) Ancient Terracottas in the British Museum,
   40 *plates,* 1810—Ancient Marbles, 6 parts, together in
   2 vol. *numerous plates, uniform half calf,* 1812-30
342 Fellows (C.) Asia Minor, *plates and cuts* 1839
343 Fellows (C.) Discoveries in Lycia, *plates, some coloured,*
   1841—Coins of Ancient Lycia, *plates,* 1855 (2)

344 Exposition Universelle de 1855 : Rapports du Jury Mixte
International, 2 vol. *and folio atlas of plates, Paris,* 1856

345 Dixon (F.) Geology and Fossils of the Tertiary and Cre-
taceous Formations of Sussex, 40 *plates, Dr. Mantell's
copy ; with autograph letter by the author* 1850

346 Sandberger (G. und F.) Die Versteinerungen des Rheinis-
chen Schichtensystems in Nassau, 39 *plates in separate
vol. half calf, Wiesbaden,* 1850-6 (2)

347 Sandberger (C. L. F.) Die Conchylien des Mainzer
Tertiärbeckens, 35 *plates, half calf* *Wiesbaden,* 1863

348 Brocchi (G.) Conchiologia Fossile Subapennina, 2 vol.
plates, uncut *Milano,* 1814

349 Visconti (E. G.) Iconographie Grecque, 3 vol. *half russia
Paris,* 1811

350 Polo (Marco) Travels, by W. Marsden, *map, half calf* 1818

351 Catalogue of the Shells contained in the Collection of
J. C. Jay *New York,* 1850

352 Hamilton (W. J.) Geology of part of Asia Minor, *plate,
being No.* 40 *of the Transactions of the Geological
Society,* 1838 (45 copies)

353 Murchison (R. I.) Silurian System, 2 parts

354 Chandler (R.) Travels in Asia Minor and Greece, 2 vol.
maps, 1817—Graham (M.) Voyage to Brazil, *plates,*
1824 (3)

355 Philippi (R. A.) Enumeratio Molluscorum Siciliæ, 2 vol.
plates *Berolini,* 1836, *&c.*

356 Montagna (C.) Giacitura del Terreno di Agnana, *coloured
and other plates, presentation copy from the author, with
autograph letter* *Napoli,* 1857

357 Reeve (L.) Conchologia Iconica, part I to XXII, *plates*
1841, *&c.*

358 Transactions of the Royal Society of Literature, 3 vol. in
6 parts, *first series, complete, plates* 1827-29

359 Lea (I.) Observations on the genus Unio, vol. III, IV, V,
plates *Philadelphia,* 1842, *&c.*

360 Lea (J.) Observations on the genus Unio, vol. III and IV,
plates *ib.* 1842, *&c.*

361 Lea (J.) Synopsis of the Family of Naiades, *ib.* 1852

362 Brander (G.) Fossilia Hantoniensia ; or Hampshire Fossils, by W. Wood, *plates on india paper* 1829

363 Krauss (F.) Die Südafrikanischen Mollusken, *plates highly
coloured* *Stuttgart,* 1848

364 Dunker (G.) Index Molluscorum, *plates, highly coloured*
Cassellis Cattorum, 1853

365 Gray (J. E.) Catalogue of Shield Reptiles, part I (Tor
toises) 49 *plates* 185

366 Le Bas (P.) Voyage Archéologique en Grèce et en Asie Mineure, *Monuments, &c.* part I to XLVI, *in roy. 4to. Architecture*, part I to XXIII (*wanting part II*) *in folio*   *Paris*, 1847-53

367 Zoology of the Voyage of H.M.S. Samarang, Mollusca 2 parts, and Vertebrata 1 part, 3 parts, *coloured plates*, 1848-9—Greenwich Magnetical and Meteorological Observations, 1866; &c.   (5)

368 Sandberger (F.) Die Conchylien des Mainzer Tertiärbeakens, part I and II, *plates*   *Wiesbaden*, 1858

369 Cellarii (C.) Notitiæ Orbis Antiqui, *front. Lipsiæ*, 1773 —Wolff (C. L. B. de) Philosophia Practica Universalis, 2 vol. *Halæ Magdeburgicæ*, 1844-50   (3)

370 Philosophical Transactions of the Royal Society, 1855, 2 parts; 1853, 3 parts; 1857, 3 parts; 1858, 2 parts; 1859, part I, *plates*   (11)

371 Palæontographical Society, vol. XX, *plates*   1866

372 Martens (G. F. V.) Merkwürdige Fälle   *Göttingen*, 1800

373 Watson (R.) Reign of Philip the Second, 2 vol.   1777

374 Bossoli (C.) War in Italy, 40 *lithographic plates*   1859

375 Luther (D. M.) Historien des Ehrwirdigen, *stamped vellum*   *Nürnberg*, 1592

376 Pindari Olympia, Nemea, Pythia, &c. Gr. cum Scholiis Græcis, *vellum*   *Romæ*, 1515

377 Pocock (W. F.) Designs for Churches and Chapels, 44 *plates*, 1835; &c.   (4)

378 Leake (W. M.) Supplement to Numismata Hellenica, 1859

379 Expédition Scientifique de Morée; Géologie et Minéralogie, par MM. P. de Boblaye, *plates, some coloured*   *Paris*, 1833

380 Soave (P.) Histoire du Concile de Trente   *Geneve*, 1635

381 Chesney (Col.) Euphrates and Tigris, the 2 Series of Maps and Charts to; and others   *a parcel*

382 Ciceronis Opera Omnia, edidit C. F. A. Nobbe, *portrait, vellum, r. e.*   *Lipsiæ*, 1850

383 Platonis Opera Omnia, Gr. edidit G. Stallbaum, *calf gilt*   *ib.* 1850

384 Aristotelis Opera Omnia, Gr. edidit C. H. Weise, *calf gilt, m. e.*   *ib.* 1843

385 Cæsar de Bello Gallico Commentarii F. Oudendorpii, *plates, old calf gilt*   *Lugd. Bat.* 1737

386 Montesquieu (M. de) Œuvres, 3 vol. *map, &c. old calf gilt*   1767

387 Sarpi (Fra-Paulo) Histoire du Concile de Trente, par P. F. le Courayer, 2 vol. *port. calf*   *Amst.* 1736

388 Milton (J.) De Doctrina Christiana, Treatise on Christian
Doctrine, by C. R. Sumner, 2 vol. *facsimiles, russia gilt*
Camb. 1825

389 Boswell (J.) Life of S. Johnson, 2 vol. *first edition, por-*
trait after Reynolds, calf 1791

390 Burney (C.) Musical Performances in Commemoration of
Handel, *plates by Bartolozzi, &c. calf* 1785

391 Bagster's Analytical Greek Lexicon 1852

392 Lucretius (T.) Nature of Things, by J. M. Good, 2 vol.
1805

393 Ainsworth's Latin Dictionary, by J. Carey 1816

394 Boiste (P. C. V.) Dictionnaire Universel, par C. Nodier,
half calf *Paris,* 1834

FOLIO.

395 Harris (W.) and S. Angell, Sculptured Metopes of Seli-
nus, *plates by H. Moses, morocco gilt* 1826

396 Thomson (J.) Castle of Indolence, *series of 12 plates by E.*
Webb, &c. - 1845

397 Prout (S.) Progressive Fragments, 24 *plates*
Ackermann, 1817

398 Prout (S.) Studies of Boats, 16 *plates* *ib.* 1816

399 Prout (S.) Studies of Cottages and Rural Scenery, 16
plates *ib.*

400 Anglo-Venetian Memorials, *engravings of seals, auto-*
graphs, &c. 1851 — Jersey and Guernsey Views, 2 vol.
plates; and 9 loose Prints

401 Bhore Ghaut Railway Incline, a series of 45 large Photographs illustrating the forming of, &c. *mounted on card-*
board

402 Dionigi (M. C.) Viaggi del Lazio, *plates* *Roma,* 1819

403 Pondocatharus (F. J. D.) Tabula Militaris Itineraria, 12
sheets, 1793; &c. (2)

404 Solis (Ant. de) Historia de la Conquista de Mexico, *front.*
FIRST EDITION *Madrid,* 1684

405 Collection of Dried Specimens of Ferns, Wild Flowers, &c.
a parcel

406 Heylyn (P.) Life of Abp. Laud, *port. by White* 1668

407 Facciolati Totius Latinitatis Lexicon, Opera Forcellini,
2 vol. *fine copy, russia, Patavii,* 1771—Appendix ad
Lexicon, *portrait, half russia, ib.* 1816 (3)

408 Milton (J.) Poetical Works, *portrait by White and plates*
1695

409 Milton (J.) Prose Works, 3 vol. *portrait by Faithorne*
Amsterdam, 1698

410 Grotii (H.) Annotationes in Libros Evangeliorum, *fine*
impression of the portrait, russia gilt *ib.* 1641

411 Nizolii (M.) Thesaurus Ciceronianus, in 2 vol. *half russia*
Basileæ, 1613
412 Epigrammatum Græcorum Libri VII, cum notis J. Bro-
daci, *vellum*   *ib.* 1549
413 Pliny (C.) Histoire du Monde, par A. du Pinet, 2 vol.
in 1   *Paris*

SECOND DAY'S SALE.

OCTAVO ET INFRA.

LOT
414 Liturgia Anglicana, 1703, with Psalms in Metre, 1708,
portrait of Q. Anne, in 1 vol.—Castellionis (S.) Dialogi,
Goudæ, 1613 — Pakington (Lady) Lively Oracles, 1682
—Ken (Bp.) Approach to the Holy Altar, 1852   (4)
415 Cicero de Officiis, Senectute et Amicitia, *Pickering's
diamond edition,* 1821—Helvetiorum Respublica, *Lugd.
Bat. Elzevir,* 1627—Terentius, edente M. Maittaire,
1713—Manutii (P.) Epistolæ, *Coloniæ,* 1572   (4)
416 Ogilvie (J.) Poems, 2 vol. 1771 — Wicamical Chaplet,
edited by G. Huddesford, 1804—Butler (S.) Hudibras,
cuts, Edinb. 1784—Gay (J.) Fables, 1812 — Gray (T.)
Works, with Life by W. Mason, 2 vol. *portraits,* 1807—
Thomson (J.) Seasons, 2 vol. in 1, *Paris,* 1803 ; and 4
others, Poetical   (12)
417 Thomson (J.) Works, with Life by P. Murdoch, 3 vol.
portraits and plates, 1788—Poetry of Anti-Jacobin and
Rejected Addresses, 2 vol. in 1, 1800-17—Sanderson
(T.) Poems, *Carlisle,* 1800—White (H. Kirke) Remains, 2 vol. *portrait, calf gilt,* 1824   (7)
418 Poe (E. A.) Poetical Works, 20 *illustrations,* 1856—
Pollok (R.) Course of Time, *portrait, Edinb.* 1846—
Beranger (P. J. de) Songs in French, with Translations
by W. Young, 1847—Crabbe (G.) Borough, 1816—
Taylor (G.) Poems, 1821   (5)
419 Byron (Lord) Lara and Jacqueline, by S. Rogers, 1814—
Don Juan, Cantos VI to XVI, 4 vol. 1824   (5)
420 Moore (T.) Epistles, Odes and other Poems, 2 vol. *frontispieces,* 1814—Poetical Works of Thomas Little, 1814—
Dictionary of Quotations (Blank Verse) 1824   (4)

421 Moore (T.) Irish Melodies, *woodcuts, calf extra, g. e.* 1823
Epistles, Odes and other Poems, 2 vol. *calf gilt*, 1817 (3)

422 Percy (Bp. T.) Reliques of Ancient English Poetry, 4 vol.
1823

423 Dryden (J.) Poetical Works, with Life by Rev. J. Mitford, 5 vol. (from Aldine Poets) *portrait*
W. Pickering, 1832-33

424 Shakspere (W.) Dramatick Writings, with Notes of all
the Commentators, 20 vol. *fine impressions of the portraits and character prints, old gilt tree-marbled calf* 1788

425 More (Sir T.) Utopia, translated by Bp. G. Burnet, 1808
— Laou-Seng-Urh, a Chinese Drama, 1817 ; and 6
others (8)

426 Horace in Latin and English, by Rev. P. Francis, 4 vol.
calf, 1750—Terence in Latin and English, by Cooke,
2 vol. 1734 (6)

427 Johnson (S.) Rambler, 3 vol. 1826—Sketches of Pictures,
Galleries in England, 1824 — Essay on Acting, *portrait
of Shakspeare,* 1828 — Instructions for a young Lady,
Edinb. 1773 — Bell (J.) Four primary Sensations, *calf,*
1852 ; and 3 others (10)

428 Cobbett (W.) French Grammar, 1824—James (G. P. R.)
History of Chivalry, 1830 — Three Months in Ireland,
1827—Formey (M.) Philosophical Miscellanies, 1759—
Montesquieu (M. de) Persian Letters, 2 vol. 1730—
Bournelle (M.) Annotations on the Tatler, 1710—
Girdlestone (C.) Parochial Sermons, *third series,* 1836 (8)

429 Coleridge (S. T.) Table Talk, *portrait* 1858

430 Coleridge (Hartley) Lives of Northern Worthies, 3 vol.
1852

431 Evelyn (J.) Life of Mrs. Godolphin, *portrait,* 1848—
Gostling (W.) Walk in and about Canterbury, *plan,
Canterbury,* 1779—Davies (Catherine) Eleven Years in
the Family of Murat King of Naples, 1841—Ellis
(Mrs. C.) on Human Nature, 1850—Gibson (W.)
Narrative of the Loss of the General Barker East-
Indiaman, with Author's Autograph Additions and
Letter (1826)—History of Thamas Kouli Kan, *portrait
and map,* 1742 (6)

432 Dickens (C.) Battle of Life, ORIGINAL EDITION, *with illustrations* 1846

433 Hoskyns (C. W.) Talpa, or Chronicles of a Clay Farm,
illustrations by G. Cruikshank, very scarce 1852

434 Mackenzie (H.) Miscellaneous Works, 3 vol. *Glasgow,*
1820— Fenelon (Archbp.) Telemachus, translated by J.
Hawkesworth, 2 vol. *plates,* 1800—Thirty Letters on
various Subjects, 2 vol. 1783 (7)

435 Hood's Comic Annual for 1832 and 1833, *humorous cuts*—
Smith (A.) Physiology of Evening Parties, *illustrations
by Leech*, 1846 (3)

436 Rousseau (J. J.) Emile, 4 vol. *plates, Amst.* 1762—Nou-
velle Heloise, 4 vol. *plates, Neuchatel,* 1764 — Lettres
écrites de la Montagne, *Amst. et Neuchatel,* 1764—
Œuvres diverses, 6 vol. *Neuchatel,* 1764 — Esprit, *portrait, ib.* 1764 16 *vol.*

437 Rousseau (J. J.) Emile, 4 vol. *plates* *Amst.* 1762

438 Cervantes (M. de) Histoire de Don Quichotte, 6 vol. *plates*
Paris, 1754

439 Davy (Sir H.) Salmonia, *woodcuts, half calf extra,* 1828—
Salter (T. F.) Angler's Guide, *portrait and cuts, half
calf gilt,* 1825 (2)

440 Chiabrera (G.) Poesie liriche, 3 vol. *Londra (Livorno)*
1781—Filacaia (V. da) Poesie, 2 vol. *ivi,* 1781—Milton
(G.) Paradiso perduto tradotto da P. Rolli, *plates,
Parigi,* 1758 (6)

441 Testament (Nouveau) *Mons,* 1762—Perrault (M.) Architecture de Vitruve en Abregé, *plates, Amst.* 1681—
Arclais de Montamy (M. d') Traité des Couleurs pour
la Peinture en Email et sur la Porcelaine, *Paris,* 1765
—Amours d'Horace, *Cologne,* 1728 — Lettres critiques
sur divers Ecrits contraires à la Religion et aux Mœurs,
par M. C***, 2 vol. in 1, *Londres (Paris)* 1751—Nadal
(Abbé) Saul, Antiochus et Mariamne, *Paris,* 1731-23-
25 ; and other Pièces de Théatre in the volume (6)

442 Etonian (The) 3 vol. 1824

443 Davies (T.) Life of D. Garrick, 2 vol. *portrait* 1780

444 Grant (J.) Great Metropolis. Both Series, 4 vol. 1838—
Random Recollections of the House of Commons. Both
Series, 3 vol. 1837-38 7 *vol.*

445 D'Açarq (M.) Observations sur Boileau, Racine, Crébillon,
Voltaire et la Langue Française en général
La Haye, 1770

446 White (G.) Natural History of Selborne, 2 vol. *plates, half
calf extra* 1825

447 Sheridan (Rt. Hon. R. B.) Works, 2 vol. *half calf extra*
1821

448 Aristophanes, translated by C. A. Wheelwright, 2 vol.
Oxford, 1837

449 Bisset (R.) Life of E. Burke, 2 vol. *half calf gilt* 1800

450 Dickens (C.) Oliver Twist, 24 *illustrations by G. Cruikshank,* 1846—Sketches by Boz. Second Series, *illustrations by G. Cruikshank,* 1837—Stanley (Dean A. P.)
Funeral Sermon on C. Dickens, 1870; with other Tracts
in the volume (3)

E

451 Virgil, translated by J. Dryden, 3 vol. *portraits and plates,* *calf* 1716
452 Scott (Sir W.) Vision of Don Roderick and other Poems, *Edinb.* 1811—Paul's Letters to his Kinsfolk, *ib.* 1816 —Chronicles of the Canongate, 2 vol. *ib.* 1827 (4)
453 Huntingdon (Selina Countess of) Life and Times, 2 vol. *portrait* 1839
454 Boaden (J.) Life of Mrs. Jordan, 2 vol. *portrait, half calf extra* 1831
455 Trials of A. Thistlewood and others for High Treason, 2 vol. 1820
456 Byron Gallery, *fine plates* 1833
457 Parker (J. H.) Hand-Book for Visitors to Oxford, 100 *woodcuts* *Oxford,* 1847
458 Irving (W.) Alhambra, 2 vol. demy 8vo. *scarce* 1832
459 Akerman (J. Y.) Coins of the Romans relating to Britain, *plates* 1844
460 Berenger (Baron de) Helps and Hints, *illustrations by G. and R. Cruikshank, Alken, &c.* 1835
461 Birmingham Riots. Letter to E. Burke from a Dissenting Attorney, *Birm.* 1791—Account of the Riots, 1791— Priestley (J.) Appeal, *ib.* 1791—Parr (S.) Sequel to Curtis, *scarce,* 1792 *in* 1 *vol.*
462 Goldsmith (L.) Secret History of the Cabinet of Bonaparte 1810
463 Watts (I.) Astronomy and Geography, 1728—Miscellanea Curiosa, 2 vol. *plates,* 1726-28 (3)
464 Hamilton (J.) Memoir of Lady Colquhoun, *portrait and view,* 1851—Klopstock and his Friends, 1814 (2)
465 Forster (C.) The one Primeval Language, 3 vol. *plates* 1852-53-54
466 Neele (H.) Lectures on English Poetry, Tales and Poems, *portrait* 1830
467 Sale (Lady) Journal of the Disasters in Affghanistan, *plans* 1843
468 Pope (A.) Temple of Fame and Messiah, with Latin Version by Usher Gahagan, confined in Newgate, *autograph of S. Pope,* 1748; and other Poems in the volume
469 Barber (T.) Picturesque Illustrations of the Isle of Wight, *views, n. d.*—Tombleson's Views on the Rhine, *plates (sold with all faults),* 1832 (2)
470 Carey (W.) Descriptive Catalogue of Sir J. F. Leicester's Collection of Paintings, LARGE PAPER 1819
471 Carter (E. J.) on Christian Grave-Stones, *plates* 1847
472 Young (E.) Night Thoughts, *half calf gilt* 1814
473 Wightwick (G.) Hints to young Architects, *woodcuts* 1846
474 Jacob (G.) Poetical Register, 2 vol. *portraits* 1723

475 Latilla (E.) on Fresco, Encaustic and Tempera Painting, *red morocco, g. e. with Her Majesty's crowned cypher in gold on sides* 1842

476 Napoleon's Book of Fate, *with folding plate*, 1826—Townshend (C. H.) Facts in Mesmerism, 1844 (2)

477 Herbert (Hon. W.) Helga, *red morocco extra, g. e.* 1815—Moile (N. T.) State Trials Specimen, 1838—Zouche (R.) Dove, *portrait, Oxford*, 1839—Reading School Poems, 1826 (4)

478 Creech (W.) Edinburgh Fugitive Pieces, *Edinb.* 1815—Beckford (W.) Recollections of an Excursion to Alcobaça and Batalha, *portrait*, 1835 (2)

479 Knight's Modern and Antique Gems, *plates* 1828

480 Percivall (W.) Anatomy of the Horse 1832

481 Gioberti (V.) on the Beautiful 1860

482 Meadows (Kenny) Heads of the People, *humorous plates, half calf gilt* 1840

483 Crowther (S.) Yoruba Vocabulary and Grammar 1852

484 Medwin (T.) Angler in Wales, 2 vol. *woodcuts* 1834

485 Bowles (W. L.) and J. G. Nichols, Annals of Lacock Abbey, *plates* 1835

486 Bridgewater Treatises, by T. Chalmers, 2 vol. *Glasgow*, 1835—J. Kidd, 1833—W. Whewell, 1834—Sir C. Bell, 1837—P. M. Roget, 2 vol. 1834—W. Buckland, 2 vol. 1836—W. Kirby, 2 vol. 1835; and W. Prout, 1834, *plates, cloth* 12 *vol.*

487 Froissart (Sir J.) Chronicles of England, France, Spain and adjoining Countries, translated by T. Johnes, 13 vol. in 12, *plates, half calf extra* 1808

488 Hume (D.) History of England, with Continuation by T. Smollett, 16 vol. *portraits and numerous engravings on copper and wood, half calf gilt* 1803-5

489 Strickland (Agnes) Lives of the Queens of England, 8 vol. demy 8vo. *portraits, uncut, scarce* 1851-52

490 Lodge (E.) Portraits of illustrious Personages of Great Britain, 12 vol. imperial 8vo. *fine impressions of the plates, calf extra* 1835

491 Angus (J.) Hand-Book, 1869—Foxe's Book of Martyrs, by T. A. Buckley, 1851—Bunyan (J.) Pilgrim's Progress, 1823—Wilson (Caroline) Autobiography, *portrait*, 1850 —Milton (J.) Poetical Works, *n. d.;* and 22 others (27)

492 Barnes (A.) on Isaiah, 3 vol. 1847-48; and 9 others by Barnes (12)

493 Works of English Puritan Divines, 8 vol. 1845-48—Doctrinal Puritans, 4 vol. 1846; and 13 others (25)

494 Dwight (T.) Theology, 5 vol. 1824; and 50 others (55)

495 Documents relating to the Settlement of the Church of England by the Act of Uniformity, 1862; &c. (26)

496 Hall (Bp. J.) Shaking of the Olive Tree, 1660—Black's
School Atlas, *Edinb.* 1846 ; and 4 others   *4to.* (6)
497 Gomez (Mad. de) La Belle Assemblée, 4 vol. *plates*, 1736
—Persian Letters, 2 vol. 1730 ; &c.   (10)
498 History of the Bucaniers of America, *portrait and plates,
scarce*   1699
499 L'Estrange (Sir J.) Fables of Æsop, &c. 2 vol. *portrait,
&c.* 1708—History of Female Favourites, 1772—Ancient
Accounts of India and China, 1733 ; &c.   (10)
500 Behn (Mrs. A.) Histories and Novels, 2 vol. *plates*, 1732-5
—Select Collection of Novels and Histories, 6 vol.
plates, 1729—Aubin (P.) Histories and Novels, 3 vol.
1739 ; &c.   (23)
501 Cervantes (M. de) Don Quixote, by P. Motteux, 4 vol.
plates, 1725—Life and Adventures of Mr. Cleveland,
Son of O. Cromwell, 5 vol. 1734—Le Sage (M.) Adventures of R. Chevalier de Beauchesne, 2 vol. 1745—
Bachelor of Salamanca, 2 vol. *plates*, 1737—Life and
Adventures of Joe Thompson, 2 vol. 1764—Guelletee,
Mogul Tales, 2 vol. *plates*, 1736 ; &c.   (26)
502 Smith (C.) Banished Man, 4 vol. 1795—Marchmont, 4 vol.
1796—Life of Harriet Stuart, 2 vol. 1751—Female
Foundling, 2 vol. 1751 ; &c.   (32)
503 Wilkins (Peter, a Cornish Man) Life and Adventures,
2 vol. *plates*, 1751—Carew (Bamfylde-Moore) Life and
Adventures, *portrait, n. d.*—Richelieu (Mlle. de) Travels
and Adventures, 3 vol. 1744 ; &c.
504 Ellis (G.) Specimens of Early English Poets, 3 vol. 1803
—Early English Metrical Romances, 3 vol. 1805, *calf,
m. e.*   *6 vol.*
505 Lee (Nath.) Dramatick Works, 3 vol. *plates*, 1734; &c. (6)
506 Manley (Mrs.) Secret Memoirs and Manners of several
Persons of Quality, from the New Atlantis, 1709—
Another edition, 2 vol. *front.* 1715-16   (3)
507 Heywood (T.) Historie of Women, the most Famous and
Infamous, *engraved title*, 1657 ; &c.   (6)
508 Mill (J. S.) Examination of Hamilton's Philosophy, 1865
— Aristotle, Politics, by R. Congreve, 1855 — Ritter
(H). et L. Preller, Historia Philosophiæ, *Gothæ*, 1864 ;
&c.   (6)
509 Carpenter (W. B.) Principles of Comparative Physiology,
300 *woodcuts*   1854
510 Butler (Bp. J.) Works, 2 vol. *portrait, calf, m. e. Oxford,*
1820—Wheatly (C.) on the Common Prayer, *ib.* 1839 ;
&c.   (7)
511 Johnson (S.) Works, by A. Murphy, 12 vol. *portrait, half
russia*   1806

512 Saltmarsh (J.) Sparkles of Glory—Goodman (J.) Old
Religion—Hill (R.) Pathway to Piety—Penitent Pilgrim—Patrick (S.) Discourse concerning Prayer, 5 vol.
calf antique, r. e.   *Pickering's reprints,* 1847-8

513 Ruskin (J.) Salsette and Elephanta, *very scarce, Oxford,*
1839; and others   (13)

514 Pulleyn (W.) Church-Yard Gleanings, and Epigrammatic
Scraps, *front. W. Upcott's copy, with autograph, several
newspaper cuttings inserted*   n. d.

515 Reed (J.) Diary of Expenses, AUTOGRAPH MANUSCRIPT,
with portrait added, 1801-4—Obituary of Poets, AUTO-
GRAPH MANUSCRIPT, *portrait added*   (2)

516 Shakespeare (W.) Life of A. Skottowe, 2 vol. *portrait,*
1824—Ireland (W. H.) Account of the Shaksperian
Manuscripts, &c. 1796; and 9 other Shaksperiana (12)

517 Abbot (Arbp. G.) Life, with Description of Guildford
Hospital, *portraits and views, Guildford,* 1777—History
of Guildford, *plates, ib.* 1801; &c.   (3)

518 Allen (B.) Chalybeat Waters of England, 1699—Blanchard
(W. C.) Charter-House, *portrait of W. Sutton added,*
1849; &c.   (10)

519 Montagu (G.) Ornithological Dictionary of British Birds,
with Additions by J. Rennie, *woodcuts*   1831

520 Marino (C.) L'Adone, 4 vol. *etchings by Le Clerc, red
sheepskin, scarce*   *D. Elsevier,* 1678

521 Klimii (N.) Iter subterraneum (Auctore L. de Holberg),
plates   *Hafniæ,* 1766

522 Kortum (C. A.) Jobsiad, translated by C. T. Brooks,
woodcuts   *Philadelphia,* 1863

523 Apulée L'Ane d'Or, 2 vol. *plates, Paris,* 1774—Boileau
(N.) Œuvres, Tome II, *La Haye,* 1722   (3)

524 Meursius Français, 2 vol. *scarce*   *Amst.* 1870

525 Quatrelles, Mille et une Nuits Matrimoniales, *Paris,* 1878
—M. Mars et Mme. Venus par le Vicomte Richard
(O'Monroy), *ib.* 1878—Monselet (C.) Amours du
Temps passé, *ib.* 1875—Pigault-Lebrun (M.) Monsieur
Botte, *cuts, ib. s. d.*   (4)

526 Chasles (P.) Mémoires, 2 vol. *Paris,* 1876-77—Gebhart
(E.) Rabelais, la Renaissance et la Réforme, *ib.* 1877—
Grisy (A. de) Histoire de la Comédie Anglaise (1672-
1707), *ib.* 1878   (4)

527 Boileau Despréaux (N.) Œuvres avec des Remarques et
des Dissertations par M. de Saint-Marc, 5 vol. *half calf
gilt, uncut*   *Amst.* 1772

528 Recueil de Pièces choisies rassemblées par les Soins du
Cosmopolite, 2 parts, *reprint (limited to 150 copies),
Anconne,* 1735—Cabinet Satyrique Tome III, *Gand,*
1860   (3)

529 Prévost (Abbé) Histoire de Manon Lescaut avec une
Préface par A. Dumas Fils, *etchings by Flameng, scarce*
Paris, 1875
530 Renard d'après un Texte Flamand du XIIᶜ Siècle edité
par J. F. Willems avec une Analyse de ce qu'ont écrit
au Sujèt par O. Delepierre *Paris*, 1837
531 Précis curieux des Hérésies, *Paris*, 1840—Paine (T.) sur
les Erreurs de G. T. Raynal, *Amst.* 1783 *in 1 vol.*
532 Procès de M. de Potter, Défenseurs M. Van Meenen et
M. Sylvain Van De Weyer, *calf extra, g. e. scarce*
Bruxelles, 1829
533 Taxes des Parties Casuelles de la Boutique du Pape avec
le Texte Latin original, *scarce* *Paris*, 1820
534 La Fontaine (J. de) Fables choisies mises en Vers, 6 vol.
in 3, *numerous engravings by Punt, Vinkeles et Delfos,
calf* *Leiden*, 1786
535 Vecellio (Cesare) Habiti antichi et moderni di tutto il
Mondo, en Italien et en Français suivis d'un Essai sur
la Gravure sur Bois par A. F. Didot, 3 vol. *numerous
plates of costume from design by* TITIAN, *scarce, especially
vol. III* (Didot's Essai) *Paris*, 1860-63
536 Tulloch (J.) Facts of Religion and of Life *Edinb.* 1877
537 Sinclair (Sir T.) Defence of Russia and the Christians of
Turkey, 2 vol. *2 maps and 9 caricatures, cloth, g. e. n. d.*
538 Lyell (Sir C.) Geological Evidences of the Antiquity of
Man, *woodcuts* 1873
539 Lytton (Lord) Works, viz.: Athens, 1874—The Student
and Asmodeus at Large, 1875—Alice, 1873—The Cax-
tons, 1874—Caxtoniana, 1875—The Disowned, 1874—
Eugene Aram, *n. d.*—Leila, Calderon, and Pilgrims of
the Rhine, 1875—Strange Story, 1875—What will he
do with it? 2 vol. 1875, *frontispieces, cloth* 11 *vol.*
540 Marco Polo's Book of the Kingdoms and Marvels of the
East, with Notes by Yule, 2 vol. *numerous illustrations*
1875
541 Milton (J.) Paradise Lost, *portrait and plates* 1808
542 Raleigh (Sir W.) Life and Letters, by E. Edwards, 2 vol.
portrait and facsimiles 1868
543 Shakespeare (W.) Dramatic Works, with Notes by Singer,
10 vol. *portrait, calf extra, g. e. by Mansell* 1868
544 Smollett (T.) Works, with Life by J. Moore, 8 vol. *port.
half calf* 1872
545 Sterne (L.) Works, 4 vol. *portrait, half calf* 1873
546 THACKERAY (W. M.) WORKS, 23 vol. *numerous illustrations*, FINE COPY *in tree-marbled calf extra, g. e.* 1869-74
547 Voyages of Adventure and Beagle, with Appendix by
Darwin, Fitzroy, and others, 4 vol. *maps and plates*, 1839
548 Wallace (A. R.) Malay Archipelago, 2 vol. *map and plates*
1867

549 Webster (N.) Improved Dictionary of the English Language, 2 vol. in 1, *portrait and plates, half calf*
Glasgow, n. d.
550 Kemble (J. P.) Memoirs, by J. A. Williams, *plates*, 1823
Authentic Narrative of Mr. Kemble's Retirement from the Stage, *portrait by Cheesman, after Lawrence, and plates*, 1817 (2)
551 Journal de la Jeunesse, 2 vol. *numerous engravings*
Paris, 1876
552 Cassell's History of England, vol. I, *illustrated*, 1857; &c. (5)
553 Minutes of Proceedings of Civil Engineers, vol. XLI and XLII, *plates* 1875
554 Racing Calendar, 1869 to 1872 4 vol.; and others (42)
555 Claudiani Opera, Varietato Lectionis illustrata ab I. M. Gesnero, 2 vol. *Lipsiæ*, 1759—Commentaires de César, 2 vol. *Lyon*, 1812; and others (17)
556 Agassiz (L.) Untersuchungen über die Gletscher, *Solothurn*, 1841, 3 *copies;* &c. (6)
557 Annales de la Société Entomologique de France, partie Supplémentaire, 1870—Haeckel (E.) Natürliche Schöpfungsgechichte, *plates, Berlin*, 1870 (2)
558 Barry (E.) Familiar Letters on a Variety of Subjects, *presentation copy from the author, very scarce, having been suppressed directly after publication* .
559 Sutherland (J.) Relations between the British Government in India and the different Native States, *map*
Calcutta, 1837
560 Bopp (F.) Grammatik der Sanskrita-Sprache, *Berlin*, 1861-3
561 Vie Privée et Publique des Animaux, *numerous clever illustrations by Grandville, half calf, m. e. Paris*, 1867
562 Ireland (S.) Miscellaneous Papers, &c. under the hand and seal of W. Shakespeare, *front. half calf* 1796
563 Whitaker (T.) Tree of Human Life, or the Bloud of the Grape 1638
564 Shee (M. A.) Rhymes on Art, 1805—Alasco, 1824 (2)
565 Bentley's Miscellany, vol. XXXIII to XL, 1853-6, *plates by J. Leech, portraits, &c. half calf* 8 *vol.*
566 Bentley's Miscellany, 47 Nos. *various*, 1851-66, *plates*, &c.
567 Clarendon (Earl of) Civil Wars in Ireland, *portrait by Kneller*, 1720—Historical Memoirs of the Irish Rebellion, 1641, &c. in 1 vol. (2)
568 Croker (T. C.) Legends of the Lakes, and Translation of Boulez-le-Gouz's Tour in Ireland, *proof sheets with author's autograph corrections, sold with all faults*
569 Fables, with Illustrations in three Languages, English by J. H. Hedley, German by F. Franke, and French by A. Dupuy, 100 *engravings* *Leipzig, n. d.*

570 Blackstone (Sir W.) Commentaries, 4 vol. *portrait, old calf gilt, Oxford*, 1775—Menin (M.) Description of the Coronation of the Kings and Queens of France, *ports.* 1775; &c. (7)

571 Luther (M.) Kleine Schriften, Nederduitsch, *port. Amst.* 1741; and others (13)

572 Miscellaneous Books *2 boxes*

573 The Holy-Days, or the Holy Feasts and Fasts, *engravings,* 1698; &c. *in 1 vol.*

574 POETS. The Works of the English Poets, with Prefaces by Dr. S. Johnson, 68 vol. (*some damaged*), *portrait, calf gilt* 1779-81

575 British Essayists, with Prefaces by A. Chalmers, 38 vol. *portraits, calf gilt, m. e.* 1823

576 Nelson (Lord) Letters to Lady Hamilton, 2 vol. *calf,* 1814; &c. *15 vol.*

577 Annual Register (Dodsley and Rivington), from commencement 1758 to 1804, with Index, 2 vol. together 49 vol. (*46 calf gilt, 3 half calf gilt*) 1758-1804

578 Stokes (J. L.) Discoveries in Australia, 2 vol. *map and plates* 1846

579 Trial of Queen Caroline, 2 vol. *portraits, &c. Smeeton,* 1820 —Memoirs of the Prince of Wales, 3 vol. 1808 *5 vol.*

580 Laurie (J.) Interest Tables, 1831—Newton (Sir I.) Natural Philosophy, by W. Davis, 3 vol. *plates,* 1803; &c. *6 vol.*

581 Frederic 2nd (King of Prussia) Posthumous Works, translated by T. Holcroft, 13 vol. *portrait, calf* 1789

582 Smith (A.) Wealth of Nations, 3 vol. 1791; &c. *11 vol.*

583 Helvetius (M.) Treatise on Man, by W. Hooper, 2 vol. 1810—Spectacle de la Nature, translated by Humphreys, 7 vol. *plates,* 1736 *9 vol.*

584 Blair (H.) Sermons, 5 vol. 1792—Another edition, 4 vol. 1794 *9 vol.*

585 Metastasio (P.) Opere Posthume, 2 vol. *half calf* *Vienna,* 1795

586 Testamentum Novum Græce, *Pickering's Diamond Edition, frontispiece* 1828

587 Homeri Ilias et Odyssea Græce, 2 vol. *Pickering's Diamond Edition* 1831

588 Catullus, Tibullus et Propertius, *Pickering's Diamond Edition* 1824

589 Dante Alighieri, La Divina Commedia, 2 vol. in 1, 1823— Petrarca (F.) Rime, *portrait,* 1822, *Pickering's Diamond Editions* (2)

590 Walton (I.) and C. Cotton's Complete Angler, *frontispiece, engraved title and woodcuts,* 1825—Walton (I.) Lives of Donne, Wotton, Hooker, Herbert and Sanderson, *front. containing ports.* 1827, *Pickering's Diamond Editions* (2)

591 Tasso (T.) Gerusalemme liberata publicata da A. Buttura,
4 vol. *portrait, calf extra*   *Parigi,* 1828
592 Shakespeare (W.) Plays, 9 vol. *Pickering's Diamond Edition*
1825
593 English Theatre, viz. Tragedies, 4 vol.—Comedies, 5 vol.—
Operas, 4 vol. together 13 vol. *half calf*   *n. d.*
594 Massinger (P.) Plays adapted for Family Reading, 3 vol.
portrait   1830-31
595 Prior (M.) Poetical Works, 2 vol. *portrait and vignette
title, calf extra,* 1825—Cowper (W.) Poems, 2 vol. *port.
calf extra,* 1824—Falconer (W.) Shipwreck, *front. and
vignette title, calf gilt,* 1823—White (H. Kirke) Poetical
Remains, 1848   (6)
596 Milton (J.) Poetical Works, with Life by Rev. J. Mitford,
3 vol. *portrait, half calf extra*   *W. Pickering,* 1834-35
597 Milton (J.) Paradise regained, *plates by Westall, calf
extra, g. e.*   1827
598 Thomson (J.) Seasons, *plates by Westall, calf gilt*   1840
599 Thomson (J.) Poetical Works, with Life by Sir N. H.
Nicolas, 2 vol. *portrait, calf extra*   *W. Pickering,* 1847
600 Young (E.) Poetical Works, 2 vol. *plates, green morocco
extra, borders of gold, g. e.*   1799
601 Waller (E.) Works, 1744—Willmott (R. A.) Pleasures,
&c. of Literature, 1854—Poems, by a Lady, *Doncaster,*
1808   (3)
602 Manners (Lord John) English Ballads, and other Poems,
scarce   1850
603 Woodrooffe (Sophia) Lethe, and other Poems, *red morocco,
g. e.*   1844
604 Palgrave (F. T.) Golden Treasury of the Best Songs and
Lyrical Poems, *calf extra, g. e.*   *Camb.* 1861
605 Tennyson (A.) Poems, *red morocco extra, g. e.*   1863
606 Tennyson (A.) In Memoriam, *blue morocco extra*   1859
607 Tennyson (A.) Princess, Maud and Idylls of the King,
3 vol. in 2, *calf extra*   1858-59
608 Tennyson (A.) Poems, 1853—In Memoriam, 1866—Enoch
Arden, &c. 1865—Maud, and other Poems, 1866—Idylls
of the King, 1867—The Princess, 1869—Holy Grail,
and other Poems, 1870   7 *vol.*
609 Langhorne (J.) Poetical Works, 2 vol. FINE PAPER, *port.
and plates, red morocco extra, borders of gold, g. e.* 1804
610 Lockhart (J. G.) Ancient Spanish Ballads, *green morocco
extra, gold tooling, g. e.*   1854
611 Gœthe (J. W. von) Faust. Beide Theile, *calf extra*
Stuttgart, 1867
612 Cruikshank (G.) Bee and the Wasp, a Fable in Verse,
etchings by G. Cruikshank, scarce   1861

613 Morris (W.) Earthly Paradise, a Poem, *fourth edition*, 1869
614 Morris (W.) Earthly Paradise, *fifth edition*, 2 vol.   1870
615 Chaucer (G.) Canterbury Tales, with Essay, Discourse,
    Notes and Glossary by T. Tyrwhitt, 5 vol. *portrait, half
    green morocco, uncut, top edge gilt*   W. Pickering, 1830
616 Percy (Bp. T.) Reliques of Ancient English Poetry, 3 vol.
    calf extra, g. e.   1839
617 Nares (E.) Heraldic Anomalies, 2 vol. *half calf*   1824
618 Rogers (S.) Italy, a Poem, *beautiful illustrations by Tur-
    ner and Stothard, red morocco, g. e.*   1830
619 Hanmer (Sir J.) Sonnets; *presentation copy to Haydon,
    with passages marked by him, and with an original sketch
    of the Artist at end*   1840
620 Westall (R.) Illustrations of Cowper's Poems, *proof plates,
    calf gilt*   1817
621 Boaden (J.) Inquiry into the Authenticity of Portraits of
    Shakspeare, *portraits*   1824
622 Beckford (W.) Excursion to Alcobaça and Batalha, *por-
    trait*   1835
623 Pennant (T.) Account of London, *plates, calf, g. e.* 1813
624 Béranger (P. J. de) Memoirs, *portrait*   1858
625 Collier (J.) Ecclesiastical History of Great Britain, 9 vol.
    half calf gilt   1845-46
626 Jowett (B.) Epistles of St. Paul to the Thessalo-
    nians, Galatians, Romans, with critical Notes and
    Dissertations, 2 vol. *uncut, scarce*   1859
627 Garrod (A. B.) Gout and Rheumatic Gout, *plates*, 1876
    —Christie (J.) Cholera Epidemics in East Africa, *maps*,
    1876— Macnamara (C.) History of Asiatic Cholera,
    1876   (3)
628 Raciborski (A.) Traité de la Menstruation, *coloured plates,
    Paris*, 1868—Churchill (F.) Principal Diseases of Fe-
    males, *engravings, Dublin*, 1844   (2)
629 Murr (C. G. von) Journal zur Kunstgeschichte und Lit-
    teratur, vol. I to XIV and XVII, 15 vol. in 8, *plates,
    Nürnberg*, 1775-89—Neues Journal, 2 vol. in 1, *plates,
    ib.* 1798-99   (9)
630 MS.   Herbarium, in Latin verse, *MS. rubricated capitals*
                                                           Sæc. xv

631 Indian Annals of Medical Science, No. IX, *Calcutta*, 1858
    —Madras Quarterly Journal of Medical Science, Nos.
    VI to XII and XIV, *Madras*, 1861-3—Second Series,
    Nos. I and II, *ib.* 1869-69—Madras Quarterly Medical
    Journal, vol. III, *ib.* 1841   (12)
632 Voltaire (M. de) Works, translated by T. Smollett, T.
    Francklin, and others, 33 vol. *portraits and plates,
    calf*,   1761-64

633 Winslow (J. B.) Sur l'Incertitude des Signes de la Mort,
2 vol.   *Paris*, 1742-45
634 Chappell (W.) Popular Music of the Olden Time, 2 vol.
facsimile   *n. d.*
635 Reynolds (G. W. M.) Mysteries of the Court of London,
6 vol. *first, third, and fourth series, 2 vol. in cloth, and
the rest in numbers*   *roy. 8vo.*   1850-6
636 Richardson (Rev. J.) Recollections, Political, Literary,
Dramatic, &c. 2 vol. in 1, *two copies*   1856
637 Richardson. The same, *two copies*   1856
638 Shakespeare (W.) Plays, edited by Manley Woods, vol. I
to IV, VI, VIII, *three copies;* IX, XII, XIII, XIV,
two copies; together 13 vol. *plates*   1806
639 Theatrical Records, *calf,* 1756—Chetwood (W. R.) General History of the Stage, 1749—Oulton (W. C.)
History of the Theatres of London, 2 vol. in 1, *calf,*
1796; and others, Theatrical   *8 vol.*
640 Gosson (S.) School of Abuse, *four copies*   1841
641 Shakespeare Society's Papers, 4 vol. *folded for binding,
two copies*   1844-9
642 Waldron, Dibdin, &c. Compendious History of the English
Stage, 1800, *three copies;* and others, *some with portraits*   *5 vol.*
643 Hone (W.) Sports and Pastimes of the People of England, *woodcuts, half calf*   1830
644 Bernard (J.) Retrospections of the Stage, 2 vol. *portrait,
uncut*   1830
645 Shakespeare (W.) Comedies, Histories, Tragedies, and
Poems, by C. Knight, *Library Edition,* vol. I, *two
copies;* II, *two copies;* VII, *two copies;* XI, *folded;*
XII, *two copies, folded;* together 9 vol.   1842
646 Shakespere (W.) Comedies, &c. by C. Knight, *National
Illustrated Edition,* Sections I to VII, and IX to
XVI, *cuts*   1852
647 Shakespeare (W.) Dramatic Works, by S. W. Singer,
2 vol. in 1, *New York,* 1836—Another, *illustrated by
A. Wivell,* in 50 numbers, *wanting part XXI, plates,
some apparently wanting, Vertue,* 1850   *2 vol.*
648 Whitlock (R.) Zootomia, or Observations on the Present
Manners of the English, *engraved front. calf*   1654
649 Walton (I.) Lives of Donne, Wotton, &c. *frontispiece*
Pickering, 1827
650 Taplin (W.) Farriery, 3 vol. *portrait,* 1796; &c.   (4)
651 Brownlow (J.) Memoranda; or Chronicles of the Foundling Hospital, *portrait of Coram, &c.* 1847—History
and Design of the Foundling Hospital, *portrait and
plates,* 1858   (2)

652 Lowndes (W. T.) Bibliographer's Manual, 6 vol. in 11
parts 1857-64

653 Pinks (W. J.) History of Clerkenwell, *imperfect*, 1865;
&c. (2)

654 Lander (R.) Records of Capt. Clapperton's Last Expedition to Africa, 2 vol. *portrait*, 1830—Matthews (H.)
Diary of an Invalid, *frontispiece*, 1835; &c. (4)

655 Britton (J.) Auto-Biography, 3 parts in 2 vol, *portraits
and other illustrations* 1850

656 Hogarth Moralized: by Dr. Trusler, *engravings, half
calf* 1841

657 Miller (T.) Our Old Town, *illustrated*, 1857; &c. (3)

658 Adams (Sir W.) New Operations for the Cataract, 1817—
Debay (A.) Hygiène et Physiologie du Mariage, *Paris,*
1873; &c. (3)

659 Burn (J. S.) History of the Fleet Marriages 1834

660 Letters from Julia to Ovid 1753

661 Irving (W.) Sketch Book, 1866; &c. (9)

662 Plays. Poor Covent Garden, 1792—Lee (R. G.) Ransom
of Manilla, 1793—Shirley (J.) Maid's Revenge, 1793;
and others, in one vol. *half calf*—Chatterton (T.) The
Revenge, *half calf*, 1795; &c. (3)

663 De Foe (D.) Journal of the Plague Year, *plates by G.
Cruikshank* 1839

664 Antiquities of London, *portraits and plates*, 1818—Grif-
fiths (R.) Jurisdiction and Conservancy of the River
Thames, 1746; &c. (4)

665 Walpole (H.) Historic Doubts of Richard III, 1822—
Foote (S.) Taste, *frontispiece*, 1752; &c. (9)

666 Harte (W.) The Amaranth, *plates*, 1767 — Ward (T.)
England's Reformation, 1716— Poems on Affairs of
State, 1697; &c. (6)

667 Chambers's Journal, vol. V to XVI, in 6 vol. *half bound*
1856-61

668 Philosophical Magazine, vol. XVIII, XIX, XX, July
1859 to Dec. 1860, 3 vol. *half calf;* &c. (7)

669 Chambers's Journal, various parts, 1866-75 *2 parcels*

670 Swift (J.) Works, 20 vol. *portraits and plates, calf*
Dublin, 1741-63

671 Brydges (Sir S. E.) Censura Literária, 10 vol. *bright old
calf gilt, scarce* 1805-9

672 Shaftesbury (Earl of) Characteristicks, 3 vol. *portrait and
vignettes by Gribelin, calf* 1727

673 England's Black Tribunall, set forth in the Trial of K.
Charles I, *portrait by Gaywood, calf* 1660

674 Stow (J.) Abridgement of the English Chronicle, black
letter, *title mounted and some leaves cut into*, 1611;
&c. (3)

675 Horne (T. H.) Introduction to the Study of Bibliography,
2 vol. *engraved facsimiles, half calf* 1814

676 Jewel (J. Bp. of Salisbury) Expositions upon the two
Epistles of the Apostle Saint Paule to the Thessalonians, black letter, *wants last leaf of Dedication, sold
with all faults* 1583

677 Wither (G.) Works, viz. Epithalamia, or Nuptiall Poems,
1620—The Shepheards Pipe, by W. Browne and G.
Wither, 1620—The Shepheards Hunting, 1620—Fide-
lia, 1620—Abuses Stript and Whipt, *woodcut,* 1617;
and another, *T. Park's copy, with his autograph notes,
to which he has added a few interesting cuttings,* in 1 vol.
sold not subject to collation

678 Paradise of Dainty Devices, edited by Sir S. E. Brydges
1810

ENGRAVINGS, PHOTOGRAPHS, &c.

679 Portrait of John Rennie, by E. Scriven, after S. Kirven,
proofs on india paper (21); &c. (23)

680 Photographs of Temples at Cairo, Nubia, &c. (7)

681 Engravings. Hulks, by Cousens, after S. Prout—Off
Calais, by Prior, after D. Cox—Rough Weather, by
Brandard, after Copley Fielding; &c. (8)

682 Boy fishing, *in oil on cardboard* (1)

683 Portrait of F. Madden, by W. Drummond (19)

684 Adoration of the Shepherds, *an oil painting in gilt frame;*
and others (4)

QUARTO.

685 Latimer (Hugh) Frutefull Sermons, black letter, *imperfect*
J. Day, 1571

686 Ascham (Roger) English Works, by J. Bennett, *calf* (1716)

687 Book of Hymns of the Ancient Church of Ireland, edited
by J. H. Todd, part I, 2 *copies* I. A. & C. Soc. 1855

688 Brayley (E. W.) Graphic and Historical Illustrator, *illustrated* 1834

689 Meteorological Papers, published by authority of the
Board of Trade, *plates,* Nos. 1 and 2 1857-8

690 Barry (Sir E.) Wines of the Ancients, *front.* 1775

691 Lomeieri (J.) De Veterum Gentilium Lustrationibus
Syntagma, *plates, vellum* Zutphaniæ, 1700

692 Montagu (G.) Testacea Britannica; or British Shells,
2 parts in 1 vol. *plates* 1803

693 Jay (J. C.) Catalogue of Shells arranged according to the
Lamarckian System, *plates* New York, 1839

694 Ducarel (Dr.) History and Antiquities of Lambeth Parish, with Appendix, *no plates, but has a few portraits, &c. added*		*Bib. Top. Brit.* 1785

695 Clementis (V.) Trinobantiados Augustæ sive Londini Lib. VI, 1636—Account of the Several Informations exhibited to the Parliamentary Committee to inquire into the Burning of the City of London, 1667 ; &c.		(3)

696 MS. Common Place Book of Extracts, by Sir S. R. Meyrick, etc. 5 vol.		1807, &c.

697 MS. Chirurgical Lectures by B. C. Brodie, 1811-12 ; and 2 others		(3)

698 MS. Winchester (H. Paulet Marq. of) Document signed for payment of allowance for riding from London to York, for 29 days		(1564)

699 Denne (J.) Shoreditch Benefactions,1777—Bartlett (F.A.) Survey of the Borough of St. Marylebone, *coloured and mounted on cloth in case, J. Britton,* 1834—Scrap Book, with cuttings respecting Lord Byron—Scrap Book, with cuttings relating to Crabbe—Yearly Meeting of Friends, *cuttings added,* 1802		(5)

700 Drew (J.) Northern Subscribers Plea re-inforc'd, *half morocco*		1651

701 Owen (R.) Report to the County of Lanark, *presentation copy with R. Southey's autograph, and having also prefixed coloured designs of proposed residence for* 2000 *persons, and R. Owen's autograph signature*		1821

702 Playfair (W.) Baronetage of England, 2 vol. 1811 — Baronetage of Ireland, 1811, *calf*		(3)

703 Willyams (C.)Voyage up the Mediterranean, *tinted plates,* 1802—Robertson (W.) America, 2 vol. 1777—History of Scotland, 2 vol. 1759		(5)

704 Davidson (E.A.) Boy Joiner and Model Maker, *illustrated, n. d.*—Sketches of Highland Character, *illustrated by W. Ralston, Edinb. n. d.*; and others		(8)

705 Parris (E. T.) Gems of Beauty, *plates*		1836

706 Ternisien d'Haudricourt, Fastes de la Nation Française, *plates*		*n. d.*

707 Norton (Hon. Mrs.) Lady of La Garaye, *portrait and view*		1862

708 Jamieson (J.) Etymological Dictionary of the Scottish Language, 2 vol. *Edinb.* 1808—Supplement to the same, 2 vol. *ib.* 1825, *uniform calf*		4 *vol.*

709 Ruskin (J.) Modern Painters, vol. I and II		1848

710 Shakespear (J.) Hindustani Selections, 2 vol. in 1, *uncut*		1840

711 Pote (J.) History and Antiquities of Windsor Castle, *plates, calf, two copies (wanting front.)*		*Eton,* 1749

712 Stephens (A. J.) Laws relating to the Clergy, vol. I, 1848—
Ecclesiastical Estates, vol. I, 1845 ; &c.		(3)

173 Novum Testamentum Græcum, *Pickering's diamond edition*		1828

714 Fitzherbert (Sir A.) La Graunde Abridgement, black letter, *title printed within borders, fine copy, calf*	1577

715 Stowe Catalogue, priced and annotated by H. R. Forster, *plates*		1848

716 Fergusson (J.) Principles of Beauty in Art, *plates and cuts*		1849

717 Shirley (J.) The Wittie Faire One, 1633—Honoria and Mammon, *interleaved 4to. size* (1659)		(2)

718 Ridpath (G.) Border History of England and Scotland, *uncut*		*Berwick*, 1848

719 Leib (K.) Resolutio Quæstionis de S. Paulo Apostolo, an conjugatus fuerit nec ne, *Ingoldstadii*, 1545—Gardineri (Stephani, Episcopi Winton) ad M. Bucerum de impudenti ejusdem Pseudologia Conquestio, *Colon.* 1845— Cochlæus(J.) de Futuro Concordiæ in Religione, *Ingolst.* 1545—Ejusdem in Musculi Anticochlæum Replica, &c. *ib.* 1545 ; and other rare Tracts by Cochlæus *in 1 vol.*

720 Modesti (J. A.) Oratio contra Lutherum, *Rhoma*, 1525— Vitelli (E.) Orationes contra Turchos, *ib.* 1518; and other rare Tracts		*in 1 vol.*

721 Scaramelli (G. B.) Il Direttorio Mistico, *Bassano*, 1840 ; and 1 other		(2)

722 Millin (A. L.) Antiquités Nationales, ou Recueil de Monumens, vol. I, *numerous plates, Paris*, 1790—Lyttelton (Lord) Historical Works, 5 vol. *calf*, 1767 ; &c.	(10)

723 Cumberland (G.) Essay on the Utility of Collecting the best Works of the ancient Engravers of the Italian School, *portrait, calf g. e.*		1827

724 Plans of various Lakes and Rivers between Lake Huron and the River Ottawa		*Toronto*, 1857

725 Novara-Expie Zoolog, Band II, *plates only*, 1864-5 ; &c.		(5)

726 Rütemeyer (L.) Der Rigi, *Basil*, 1877 ; &c.		(5)

727 Robertson (W.) History of Charles 5th, 3 vol. 1769— History of America, 2 vol. 1777—Ancient India, 1 vol. 1791		6 *vol.*

728 Cook (Capt.) First Voyage, 3 vol. *plates, &c. calf*, 1785— Bruce (J.) Travels, 5 vol. (*wants vol. III*), 1790	(7)

729 Portlock (N.) Voyage round the World, *plates*, 1789— Dixon (G.) Voyage to America, *ib.* 1789		2 *vol.*

730 Pinkerton (J.) Collection of Voyages and Travels, 17 vol. (*wanting vol.* 14), *plates*		1808-14

731 MS. Dibdin (T.) Metrical History of England, vol. I, *the original autograph MS. portraits and plates*

732 Biblia Græca, Vetus Testamentum ex Versione LXX
Interpretum curante L. Bos, *map, vellum Franeq.* 1709
733 Bible (Breeches) *woodcuts, sold with all faults* 1599
734 Bible (Holy) with Observations by Rev. Mr. Ostervald,
plates 1798
735 Pugin (A. W.) True Principles of Pointed or Christian
Architecture, *plates* 1841
736 Helvetius on the Mind, *old gilt calf* 1759
737 Horatii Opera cum Notis G. Baxteri, J. M. Gesneri, et
J. C. Zeunii, LARGE PAPER, *red morocco* *Edinb.* 1861
738 Sallustius et Florus, *Baskerville's fine edition, red morocco, g. e.* *Birm.* 1773
739 Catullus, Tibullus et Propertius, *Baskerville's fine edition,
russia* *Birm.* 1772
740 Opie (J.) Lectures on Painting, *portrait* 1809
741 Walton (I.) Lives of Donne, Wotton, Hooker, Herbert
and Sanderson, with Notes and Life of the Author by
T. Zouch, *portraits and views* *York*, 1796
742 Hayley (W.) Essay on History, Triumphs of Temper, and
other Poems, 1780-81 — Goldsmith (O.) Traveller,
Deserted Village, Retaliation and Haunch of Venison,
portrait, 1774-76 (2)
743 Hill (G.) Account of the Macdonalds of Antrim
Belfast, 1873
744 Malkin (B. H.) Scenery, Antiquities and Biography of
South Wales, *map and views by Laporte* 1804
745 Gray (Rev. J. H.) Auto-Biography, *portraits and view,
cloth, g. e. printed for private circulation* 1868
746 Book of the Illustrious, 13 *fine portraits* 1845
747 Cleland (J.) Description of the Glasgow Banquet to Sir
R. Peel, Bart. *plates* *Glasgow,* 1837
748 Graham (H. D.) Antiquities of Iona, *map and plates* 1850
749 Lee (J. E.) Isca Silurum: or an illustrated Catalogue of
the Caerleon Museum of Antiquities, *plates* 1862
750 Antiquarian Etching Club's Publications, 2 vol. *plates*
1849-50
751 Johnson (S.) Rasselas, *engravings by Raimbach from pictures by Smirke* 1805
752 Fenelon (Archbp.) Telemachus, translated by J. Hawkesworth, 2 vol. in 1, *fine plates by Stothard, russia,* 1795
753 Smith (J. T.) Antiquities of London, *plates* 1791
754 Gerning (J. J. von) Picturesque Tour along the Rhine,
coloured views 1820
755 Thorndike (H.) Just Weights and Measures 1662
756 Sotheby (W.) Tour through Wales, and other Poems,
views by J. Smith 1794
757 Fenton (R.) Historical Tour through Pembrokeshire,
portrait and plates 1811

FOLIO.

758 Burnet (Bp. G.) History of his own Time, 2 vol. *uncut*
1724-34

759 Report on Miscellaneous Expenses, 1848—Report on
Salaries, &c. 1849 (2)

760 Ireland. Various Documents, with Autograph Signatures
of Lords Lieutenants (Rutland, Westmoreland, Nugent,
Buckingham, Northington, Nugent Temple, Lifford, &c.)
with Copies of Instructions, MANUSCRIPTS *a parcel*

761 Ireland. Map of St. Patrick's Brewery, *drawing on
vellum, by M. Fitzgerald*—Plan of part of Wilsfort, by
J. W. Wright, *drawing, dated* 1835—Various old In-
dentures, Autograph Letters respecting Property—
Answer of J. Dumas against the Complaint of J. Whit-
ing, of Cork; &c. *a parcel*

762 Characters, Scenes, &c. for Toy Theatres, *mostly coloured,
a large quantity* 3 *parcels*

763 Mendez Pinto (Fernand) Voyages and Adventures, by H.
C(ogan) 1653

764 Caserta. Dichiarazione dei Disegni del Reale Palazzo di
Caserto, *plates* *Napoli,* 1756

765 Vetusta Monumenta, vol. IV, *plates, half calf* 1815

766 Guerrazzi (G. B.) Vedute di Livorno, *plates oblong.* 1814

767 Heywood (T.) Nine Bookes of various Historie concern-
inge Women, *wants title, &c. sold not subject to return,*
1826—Book of Common Prayer, black letter, *imperfect* (2)

768 Guildford. History and Description of Guildford, *inlaid
and illustrated with scarce views, Guildford,* 1777—
Guildford Poll Book, *ib.* 1858—Rowe (J.) Twelve Views
of Guildford, *Dorking, n. d.;* and Sundry Engravings,
Bills, Cuttings from Newspapers, &c. *in a Solander case*

769 Ayliffe (J.) Commentary, by way of Supplement to the
Canons and Constitutions of the Church of England,
calf, r. e. 1726

770 Scapulæ (J.) Lexicon Græco-Latinum, *calf gilt*
Oxonii, 1820

771 Stuart (J.) and N. Revett, Antiquities of Athens, 3 vol.
plates, sold with all faults 1762-95

772 Rossi (D. de) Raccolta di Statue antiche e moderne, *plates,
imperfect* *Roma,* 1742

773 William III. Komste van Zyne Majesteit in Holland,
portrait and plates *Graavenhaage,* 1691

774 Hopper (T.) Designs for the Houses of Parliament,
plates, half morocco *n. d.*

775 Davis (E.) Gothic Ornaments of Prior Birde's Oratory in
Bath Abbey, No. I, *plates,* 1834—Examples of Building
Constructions, 4 Nos. *plates* (5)

776 Rossini's La Donna del Lago, Italian and German Words
  for Voice and Pianoforte, *Leipzig;* and others, chiefly
  . modern Pianoforte Music   *a parcel*
777 Pettet (A.) Original Sacred Music—Handel's Funeral
  and Wedding Anthems, full scores, in 1 vol. *frontis-*
  piece by Bartolozzi   **2 vol.**
778 Stanley (T.) History of Philosophy, *portrait by Faithorne*
          1701
779 Milton (G.) Paradiso perduto, Traduzione di P. Rolli,
  portraits   1736
780 Stuart (J.) and N. Revett, Antiquities of Athens, vol. I,
  plates   1762
781 Collection of Theatrical Puffs, Play-Bills, &c. both London and Provincial, in a Scrap Book
782 Andrewes (Bp. L.) XCVI Sermons   1631
783 Andrewes (Bp. L.) XCVI Sermons   1632
784 Homilies, black letter   1673
785 Ecclesiastical Histories by Eusebius, Socrates, Evagrius
  and Dorotheus, translated by M. Hanmer   1619
786 Lucian, translated by J. Mayne and F. Hicks, *Oxford,*
  1664—Tacitus, translated by R. Greenway, 1622   (2)
787 Machiavell (N.) on Wel Governing   1662
788 Dugdale (Sir W.) Monasticon Anglicanum epitomized,
  plates   1693
789 Stukeley (W.) Itinerarium curiosum. Centuria I, *plates,*
  sold with all faults   1724.
790 Brand (L.) Cris de Vienne, &c. 42 *plates*   *Vienne,* 1775
791 Domesday Book of Gloucestershire and Sussex, 2 vol.
  photo-zincograph facsimiles   1862
792 Pinelli (B.) Cinquanta Costumi Pittoreschi, 50 *etchings,*
  half morocco   *Roma,* 1809
793 Ottley (W. Y.) Collection of 39 Facsimiles of rare Etchings, *plates on india paper, half morocco*   1828
794 Canova (A.) Works, 2 vol. LARGE PAPER, *portrait and*
  engravings in outline by H. Moses, half russia   1824
795 Camden (W.) Britannia, with large Additions by Bp. E.
  Gibson, 2 vol. *portrait, maps and plates*   1753
796 Bingham (J.) Works, 2 vol.   1726
797 HOUBRAKEN AND VERTUE'S HEADS OF ILLUSTRIOUS
  PERSONS, with Lives by T. Birch, 2 vol. in 1, *fine*
  portraits   1747-52
798 GALLERIA PITTI, illustrata per Cura di L. Bardi, 4 vol. in 8,
  numerous beautiful engravings, maroon morocco extra,
  gold tooling, g. e. by G. Sardi of Leghorn, AN ORIGINAL
  SUBSCRIBER'S COPY   *Firenze,* 1837-42
799 Sarpi (Fra Paulo) Histoire du Concile de Trente, par P.
  F. Le Courayer, 2 vol. *portrait, uncut*   1736
800 Locke (J.) Works, 3 vol. *portrait, wormed*   1722

801 Collins (G.) Great-Britain's Coasting Pilot, *large plans*
1781
802 Pope (A.) Essay on Man, part I, *first edition*, 1732—First
Satire on the Second Book of Horace, *ib.* 1733—Of the
Use of Riches, *ib.* 1732—Of the Characters of Women,
ib. 1735—Duck (S.) The Vision, 1737 ; &c.   *in 1 vol.*
803 Ten Lithographic Coloured Flowers, by a Lady, *Edin.* 1826
804 Money Market Review, vol. XXIV to XXVII, 1872-3, &c.
805 Play-Bills, Posters, Tickets, &c. of various London and
Provincial Theatres, Concert Rooms, &c. *many relating
to Covent Garden Theatre, Drury Lane, The Argyle
Rooms, &c. collected by J. N. Burns, Editor of Beaufoy's
Tokens*   *a parcel*
806 Cuttings from Illustrated Papers —Athenæum, various
Nos. ; &c.   *3 parcels*
807 Report of the Sepulchral Monuments Committee, 1872,
not published—Wright (T.) on the Legend of Weland
the Smith, 1848 ; and others   *various sizes.* (20)
808 Miller (P.) Gardener and Botanist's Dictionary, by T.
Martyn, 4 vol. *russia, m. e.*   1807
809 Sandys (G.) Description of Turkey, Egypt, the Holy Land,
&c. *plates*, 1637 ; and others   *3 vol.*
810 Fuller (T.) Historie of the Holy Warre, *no frontispiece or
map*   1639
811 Chronicon Nurembergense (Auctore H. Schedel), *numerous fine woodcuts, first few leaves neatly mended, and
stained at end, sold therefore with all faults,Augusta,* 1497

THIRD DAY'S SALE.

OCTAVO ET INFRA.

LOT
812 Hall (S. T.) Days in Derbyshire, 60 *illustrations*, 1863—
Murray's Handbook for Ireland, *map*, 1864—Cliffe (C.
F.) Book of S. Wales, *illustrated*, 1847; and others (28)
813 Otto (E.) German Conversation-Grammar, *Leipzig*, 1870
—Smith (W.) Principia Latina, part II and III—Collier
(W. F.) History of the British Empire, 1871—Colenso
(J. W.) Arithmetic, 1870 ; and others   (18)
814 School Books (Modern) various   (56)

815 Flügel's German and English Dictionary, 1857—Baedeker's
Manual of Conversation, *Coblenz*, 1858 ; &c.   (8)
816 Sadler (P.) Dictionnaire Anglais-Français et Français-
Anglais   *Paris*, 1864
817 Tarver (J. C.) Royal Phraseological English-French and
French-English Dictionary, 2 vol. *half calf*   1853
818 Baretti's Italian and English Dictionary, by J. Davenport
and G. Cornelati, 2 vol.   1860
819 Flügel's Complete Dictionary of the German and English
Languages, by C. A. Freiling and A. Heimann, 2 vol. 1843
820 Koehler (F.) German and English Dictionary, 2 parts in
1 vol. 1865—Smith (W.) Smaller Latin-English Dictionary, 1871   (2)
821 Walker's Critical Pronouncing Dictionary, by J. Davis,
portrait, 1840—Boyer and Deletanville's French and
English Dictionary, 1835 ; &c.   (4)
822 Gibbon (E.) Roman Empire, 12 vol. *portrait and maps,*
half calf   1820
823 Macfarlane (C.) and T. Thomson, Comprehensive History
of England, 4 vol. in 12 divisions, *over* 1000 *engravings*
1861
824 Hume (D.) and T. Smollett, History of England, with
Continuation by W. Jones, 20 vol. *vignette titles, half*
morocco   *Chiswick Press*, 1828
825 Buckle (H. T.) History of Civilization in England, 2 vol.
1861
826 Motley (J. L.) History of the United Netherlands, 2 vol.
portraits and map   1860
827 Motley (J. L.) Rise of the Dutch Republic, 3 vol.   1856
828 Pope (A.) Works, by W. Roscoe, 10 vol. *portraits and*
faasimile, half morocco, m. e.   1824
829 Lodge (E.) Portraits of Illustrious Personages of Great
Britain, 8 vol. *portraits*   1849
830 Alison (A.) History of Europe, 20 vol. and Atlas, 1847-
1848   (21)
831 Alison (A.) History of Europe, 1815-52, 9 vol. and Epi-
tome Atlas   1852-9
832 Alison (A.) Essays, Political, Historical and Miscellaneous,
3 vol.   1850
833 Landor (W. S.) Imaginary Conversations of Greeks and
Romans, 1853—Carlyle (T.) Chartism—Abercrombie
(J.) Intellectual Powers, 1849 — Moral Feelings, 1849
—Essays and Tracts, *Edinb.* 1847 : &c.   (7)
834 Conybeare (W. J.) Essays, Ecclesiastical and Social, 1855
—Foster (T. C.) Letters on the Condition of the People
of Ireland, 1847—Hannay (J.) Essays from " The
Quarterly Review," 1861 ; &c,   (4)

835 Hessey (J. A.) Sunday (Bampton Lectures, 1860), 1861—
Temple (F.) Rugby Sermons, 1858-60-61—Essays and
Reviews, 1861 (3)
836 Cockburn (Lord) Life of Lord Jeffrey, 2 vol. *portrait*
Edinb. 1852
837 Clarendon (E. Earl of) History of the Rebellion, *Ox.* 1843
838 Prichard (J. C.) Natural History of Man, *over 150 coloured
and other illustrations* 1848
839 Pickering (C.) Races of Man, *plates*, 1850—Manual of
Geographical Science, Mathematical, &c. 1859—Hunt
(R.) Manual of Photography, *illustrated*, 1857; &c. (5)
840 Spectator (The) *portraits*, 1846—Shakespeare (W.) Dramatic Works, *portrait* (2)
841 Plutarch's Lives, by J. and W. Langhorne, 1841—Carlyle
(A.) Autobiography, *portrait*, 1860; &c. (3)
842 Wellington (Duke of) Life of, by an Old Soldier, *illustrated by A. Cooper*, 1852—Maxwell (W.) Victories of
Wellington, &c. *portraits, &c.* 1852 (2)
843 Richardson (J.) Travels in the Great Desert of Sahara,
2 vol. *fronts. and map*, 1848—Keppel (H.) Expedition to
Borneo of H.M.S. Dido, 2 vol. *plates*, 1846—Coulter
(J.) South America, 2 vol. 1847 (6)
844 Dickens (C.) Pickwick Papers, *plates by R. Seymour and
Phiz, few leaves torn, all faults* 1837
845 Dickens (C.) David Copperfield, *illustrated by H. K.
Browne, uncut* 1850
846 Dickens (C.) Dombey and Son, *illustrated by H. K. Browne,
uncut* 1848
847 Netherclift (F. G.) and R. Sims, Hand-book of Autographs, 1862—Snell (H. J.) Enamel Painting on Glass,
China, &c. *coloured and other illustrations*—Reynolds
(Sir J.) Discourses, *half calf*, 1778; &c. (5)
848 Sala (G. A.) Seven Sons of Mammon, 1864—Barren
Honour, 1866; and others (7)
849 Standard Library Cyclopædia, 4 vol. 1848—Sismondi (J.
C. L. S. de) Literature of the South of Europe, 2 vol.
portraits, 1846 *Bohn* (6)
850 Sheridan (R. B.) Dramatic Works, *portrait*, 1848—Roscoe
(W.) Life of Lorenzo de Medici, *port.* 1846—Schiller
(F.) Thirty Years War, *ib.*—De Vigny (Count A.)
Cinq-Mars, by M. Hazlitt, *port.* 1847; and others (7)
851 Shakespeare (W.) Works, by W. Warburton, 8 vol. *portrait* 1747
852 Gurwood (Lt. Col.) Selections from the Wellington Despatches, 1851—Henegan (Sir R. D.) Seven Years Cam-
paigning in the Peninsular, &c. 2 vol. 1846—Hodson
(W. S. R.) Twelve Years of a Soldier's Life in India,
portrait, 1859 (4)

853 Sturm (C. C.) Reflections, *portrait*, 1837—Short (T. V.)
 History of the Church of England, 1855—Melvill (H.)
 Sermons, 2 vol. *half morocco*, 1845—Bowdler (J.) Select
 Pieces, 2 vol. *portrait, calf*, 1816 ; &c. (8)
854 Stevenson (W. F.) Praying and Working, 1862—Brewster
 (D.) More Worlds than One, 1854—Barrington (A.)
 Lectures on Heraldry, *plates*, 1844 (6)
855 Footsteps of St. Paul, *illustrated*, 1860—Winslow (O.) No
 Condemnation in Jesus Christ, 1857—Helmore (T.)
 Manual of Plain Song, 1850—Hook (W. F.) Christian
 Thought, 2 vol. *Leeds*, 1850 ; and others (17)
856 Todhunter (I.) Algebra, 1870—Smith (B.) Arithmetic,
 1868—Roscoe(H. E.) Lessons in Elementary Chemistry,
 illustrated, 1871; and others (6)
857 Sala (G. A.) Lady Chesterfield's Letters to her Daughter,
 1860; and others (30)
858 Brookes (R.) General Gazetteer, *maps*, 1842—Government Ordnance Map of the Country round Bath, *large
 sheet mounted on linen ;* &c. (3)
859 Beeton (Mrs.) Book of Household Management, *illustrated*,
 1864—Men of the Time, 1853 ; &c. (4)
860 Henry (W.) Experimental Chemistry, 2 vol. 1829—Imison
 (J.) Elements of Science and Art, 2 vol. 1808—Williams
 (J.) Natural History of the Mineral Kingdom, 2 vol.
 Edinb. 1810; &c.
861 Johnston (A. K.) School Atlas of Classical Geography,
 1861—Donnegan (J.) Greek and English Lexicon, 1826
 —Lord (J.) School History of Modern Europe; &c. (11)
862 Hemans (Mrs.) Siege of Valencia, *calf*, 1823—Spirit of the
 Metropolitan Conservative Press, vol. II, 1840 ; &c. (18)
863 Good Words, for 1866—Sunday at Home, for 1868 ; and
 others (18)
864 Testament (New) in Greek, with English notes by
 E. Valpy, 3 vol. *calf extra* 1826
865 Testament (New) in Greek, with English notes by S. T.
 Bloomfield, 2 vol. in 1, *half calf* 1836
866 Scripture Treasury, *S. Bagster, n. d.*—Bickersteth (E.)
 on the Prophecies, and on Baptism, 2 vol. 1839-40—
 Evans (R. W.) Ministry of the Body, 1851; and 20
 others, Religious (24)
867 Krummacher (F. W.) Elisha, *Cheltenham*, 1838—Hanna
 (W.) Last Day of Our Lord's Passion, *Edinb.* 1864—
 Bridges (C.) on Psalm CXIX, 1830—Churton (E.)
 Early English Church, 1840—Pearson (T.) on Infidelity, *n. d. ;* and 20 others, Religious (25)
868 Jackson (Bp. J.) Sinfulness of little Sins, 1854—Keith
 (A.) on Prophecy, *cuts, calf, Edinb.* 1833—Hirscher
 (J. B. von) Proposals for a New Reformation, with

notes by A. C. Coxe, *Oxford*, 1852—Law (W.) Serious
Call, 1824—O'Sullivan (M.) Guide to an Irish Gentleman in his Search for a Religion, *Dublin*, 1833—Juelli
(J.) Apologia Ecclesiæ Anglicanæ, *an Edition unknown
to Lowndes*, 1584; and 10 others, Religious   (16)

869 Taylor (Bp. J.) Holy Living and Dying, 1719—Burnet
(Bp. G.) on the XXXIX Articles, *Edinb.* 1745 —
Wheatly (C.) on the Book of Common Prayer, 1722—
Edwards (J.) Veritas redux, 1707—Tong (W.) Life of
M. Henry, *portrait*, 1716—Wilkins (Bp. J.) on Prayer,
1704; and 6 others, Religious   (12)

870 Shepherd (J.) on the Book of Common Prayer, 2 vol. 1817
—Pearson (Bp. J.) on the Creed, 2 vol. *portrait, Oxford*, 1797—Hodgson (C.) Instructions to the Clergy,
1838   (5)

871 Taylor (I.) Spirit of the Hebrew Poetry, 1861—Horne
(Bp. G.) on the Psalms, 2 vol. *Oxford*, 1798—Oliver
(P.) Scripture Lexicon, *ib.* 1810 — Adams (Hannah)
History of the Jews, 1818   (5)

872 Faber (G. S.) Difficulties of Infidelity, 1824—Bean (J.)
Family Worship, 1826, with other Tracts in the Volume
—De Courcy (R.) Christ Crucified, 1810—Conference
Missions at Liverpool, 1860—Unitarianism confuted,
Liverpool, 1839   (5)

873 Tyerman (L.) Oxford Methodists, *portraits*, 1873—Luther
(M.) on Galatians, *portrait*, 1807—Answer to the Case
of the Dissenters, 1834—Bridges (C.) Christian Ministry, 1835—Baxter (R.) Reformed Pastor, 1825   (5)

874 Gunning (Bp. P.) Lent Fast, *calf extra*   *Oxford*, 1845

875 Newman (J. H.) Lectures on Justification   1838

876 Eaton (J. R. T.) Permanence of Christianity (Bampton
Lectures) 1873—Shuttleworth (Bp. P. N.) Sermons on
the Principles of Christianity, *Oxford*, 1827—Guizot
(F.) Meditations on Christianity, 1864—Blunt (J. H.)
Christian View of Christian History, 1866   (4)

877 Walker (S.) Sermons, 2 vol. 1763—Pentycross (T.) Sermons, 1781 — Fawcett (J.) Sermons, 2 vol. *Carlisle*,
1817—Fanch (J.) Sermons, 1768   (6)

878 Burgon (Dean J. W.) on the Pastoral Office, 1864 —
Browne (J. H.) Charge against Oxford Tracts, 1838—
Heurtley (C. A.) University Sermons, *Oxford*, 1862 (3)

879 Palmer (W.) Treatise on the Church, 2 vol.   1842

880 Ecclesiastical History Society's Publications, viz. Wood
(A. a) Life, *Oxford*, 1848—Field (R.) of the Church,
4 vol. *Camb.* 1847-52 — Book of Common Prayer for
Ireland, 3 vol. 1849-50 — Strype (J.) Memorials of
Archbp. Cranmer, 3 vol. in 4, *Oxford*, 1848-54—Heylyn
(P.) History of the Reformation, 2 vol. *Camb.* 1849, 14 *vol.*

881 Homilies, *Oxford*, 1840—De Courcy (R.) Sermons, *portrait*, 1810—Hughes (J.) Sermons, *Aberystwyth*, 1843 —Scottish Pulpit, vol. IV, *portrait*, *Glasgow*, 1835   (4)

882 Pulpit (The) 16 vol. *portraits*   1824-31

883 Beveridge (Bp. W.) on the XXXIX Articles, *Oxford*, 1847—Burnet (Bp. G.) on the XXXIX Articles, *ib.* 1831 — Wilson (W.) on the XXXIX Articles, *ib.* 1840   (3)

884 Graves (Dean R.) Works, 4 vol. *portrait*   1840

885 Mosheim (J. L.) Ecclesiastical History, 1839—Milner (J.) Church History, *Edinb.* 1838   (2)

886 Lendrum (A.) Principles of the Reformation, 1875 — Luther (M.) on Galatians, *portrait*, 1832—Churchman's Magazine, 2 vol. 1853   (4)

887 Paul (St.) Epistles to the Thessalonians, Galatians and Romans, with Notes and Dissertations by Rev. B. Jowett, 2 vol. *scarce*   1859

888 Scrivener (F. H.) Exact Transcript of the Codex Augiensis, a Græco-Latin Manuscript of S. Paul's Epistles. To which is added a Collation of 50 Manuscripts, *facsimiles*   *Camb.* 1859

889 Good Words for 1868 and 1869, edited by N. Macleod, 2 vol. *numerous illustrations, half bound*   1868-69

890 Lives of E. Pocock, Bp. Pearce, Bp. Newton, and Rev. P. Skelton, 2 vol.   1816

891 Donnegan (J.) Greek and English Lexicon, 1837—Middleton (Bp. T. F.) on the Greek Article, *Camb.* 1828; and others   (8)

892 Homeri Ilias, Gr. et Lat. cum notis S. Clarke, 2 vol. 1815; and 10 other Greek Classics   (12)

893 Herodotus, Græce, 2 vol. *Oxon.* 1814—Herodotus, translated by I. Littlebury, 2 vol. 1737   (4)

894 Euripides. Four Plays in English Prose from Porson's Text, *Oxford*, 1820—Sophocles, translated by R. Potter, 1820—Xenophon's Expedition of Cyrus, &c. translated by E. Spelman, 1811—Terence, Englished by L. Echard, 1729   (4)

895 Velleius Paterculus, *Lugd. Bat. Elzevir*, 1639 — Livius, curante M. Maittaire, 6 vol, 1722—Juvenalis et Persius, 1720—Horatii Epistolæ ad Pisones et Augustum, with English Commentary by Bp. R. Hurd, 3 vol. 1766 —Horatius Delphini, *wants title*   (12)

896 Horatius, Martialis et Terentius, cum notis variorum, 3 vol.   *Lugd. Bat.* 1670-56-69

897 Whately (Archbp. R.) Logic, 1840—Watts (I.) Logick and Philosophical Essays, 2 vol. 1731-63 — Book of Science, 1833; and 2 others   (6)

898 Bridge (B.) Algebra, with Key, 2 vol. 1831-24—L. U. K.
Geometry, 1830—Simson (R.) Parent's Guide, 1838 (4)

899 Locke (J.) on the Human Understanding, 2 vol. *portrait*,
1741—Prideaux (H.) Life of Mahomed and Right of
Tithes, 2 vol. in 1, 1718-10—Voltaire's Henriade, 1732
—Worgan (J. D.) Poems, *portrait*, 1810 (5)

900 Kitchiner (W.) Art of prolonging Life, 1828—Cabinet
Lawyer, 1859; and 14 others (16)

901 Sherer (M.) Life of Duke of Wellington, 2 vol. 1830—
Galt (J.) Life of Lord Byron, *portrait*, 1830—Burnet
(Bp. G.) Life of Sir M. Hale, *portrait*, 1682—Life of
Olympia Morata, 1834—Walton (I.) Lives, 1819; and
4 others (10)

902 Rollin (C.) Belles Lettres, 4 vol. 1770—Knox (V.) Essays,
2 vol. 1778; and 2 others (8)

903 Phillips (H.) Sylva Florifera, 2 vol. 1823

904 White (G.) Natural History of Selborne, *Edinb.* 1833—
Letters from Ireland, by Charlotte Elizabeth, 1838;
and 6 others (8)

905 Bingley (W.) Animal Biography, 4 vol. *plates*, 1820—
Insect Architecture, *woodcuts*, 1830—Architecture of
Birds, *woodcuts*, 1831 (6)

906 Zincke (F. B.) Egypt of the Pharaohs and of the Khedive,
1871—Russell (M.) Ancient and Modern Egypt, *map
and woodcuts, Edinb.* 1831 (2)

907 Westgarth (W.) Colony of Victoria, 1864—Booth (E. C.)
Another England: Life in Victoria, 1869—Yate (W.)
Account of New Zealand, *portrait and plates*, 1835—
Greenwood (F. W. P.) History of King's Chapel,
Boston, the first Episcopal Church in New England,
view, Boston, 1833 (4)

908 Folengo (T.) Orlandino di Limerno Pitocco, *woodcuts, last
leaf damaged, sold with all faults, rare Vinegia*, 1550

909 Folengo. Another Edition, *engraved title by Moreau,
scarce Londra (Parigi)* 1773

910 Dante con nuove Ispositioni, *woodcuts, Lyone,* 1552—
L'Amoroso Convivio, *Vinegia*, 1531—Satire di cinque
Poeti (Ariosto, Sansovino, Bentivogli, Alamanni, e
Paterno) *Venetia*, 1565—Philoxeno (Marcello) Stram-
moti e Sonetti, *ivi*, 1507 (4)

911 Historia del felice Innamoramento del Delfino di Francia
et di Angelina Loria, nobile Siciliana, *a rare Romance
of Chivalry, in Prose, Venetia*, 1562—Libro chiamato
Falconetto, *Romance of Chivalry in ottava Rima, woodcuts, wants one, s. l. & a.* (2)

912 Boccaccio (G.) Decamerone, *Vinegia*, 1552—Argelati (F.)
Decamerone, 2 vol. *Bologna*, 1751—Grazzini detto il

H

Lasca (A. F.) Novelle, *uncut*, 1756—Giraldi (G.)
Novelle, *morocco*, *Amst.* 1819—Conto de Conti, *woodcuts*, *Napoli*, 1769 (6)

913 Tasso (T.) Gerusalemme Liberata con un Discurso critico
di Ugo Foscolo, *Firenze*, 1853—Manfredi (E.) Rime,
portrait, *Bologna*, 1748 — Guidiccione (G.) Rime e
Prose, *Napoli*, 1720— Lippi (L.) Il Malmantile rac-
quistato, *engraved title by Moreau and portrait*, *Parigi*,
1768—Marini (Cav. G. B.) La Strage degl' Innoenti,
portraits of the Duke of Alva and Marini,, *Napoli*, 1632
Bergamo (Andrea da) Satire alla Carlona, 2 vol. in 1,
Venetia, 1566 (6)

914 Celestina Tragicomedia de Calisto et Melibea tradotta in
Italiano, *woodcuts*, *Venetia*, *Sabio*, 1541—Bistricci (R.)
Campagnia della Bastina, *woodcut*, *Pavia*, 1597—Croce
(G. C. della) Bertoldino e Bertoldo, 2 vol. in 1, *Mi-
lano, s. a.* (3)

915 Gianni (F.) Poesie, 2 vol. *morocco, g. e.*   *Milano*, 1807

916 Doni (A. F.) La Zucca, ORIGINAL EDITION, *uncastrated*,
woodcuts, rare   *Vinegia, Marcolini*, 1551-52

917 Doni (A. F.) La Zucca espurgata da Jeronimo Gioan-
nini, *three Editions* .   *Venetia*, 1589-91-1607

918 Castiglione (Sabba) Ricordi, *title wanting, but supplied
from Edition of Venetia, 1565, calf gilt, Milano*, 1561—
Ambasciata di Romolo á Romani, *Bruselles*, 1671 —
Pescetti (O.) Proverbi Italiani, *Venetia*, 1603 (3)

919 Savonarola (H.) della Vita Christiana   *Venetia*, 1547

920 Bembo (P.) Gli Asolani, *Vinegia, Aldo*, 1575—Sannazaro
(I.) Arcadia, *ivi, Aldo*, 1514   *in one vol.*

921 Dolce (L.) Dialogo del Modo di accrescere et conservar la
Memoria, *curious woodcuts*   *Venetia*, 1586

922 Magi (G.) Guerra di Fiandra (in ottava Rima) *Vinegia*,
1551—Zazzaroni (P.) Giardino di Poesie, *plates, Verona*,
1641—Dante Alighieri Purgatorio, in Versi e in Prosa,
Firenze, 1849 (3)

923 Giraldi Cinthio (G. B.) Tragedie, *woodcut portrait to each*,
Venetia, 1583—Beolco detto Il Ruzante (A.) Opere,
Vicenza, 1584 (2)

924 Sestini (D.) Lettere scritte dalla Sicilia e della Turchia,
4 vol. in 2   *Firenze*, 1779-81

925 Filangieri (G.) Scienza della Legislazione ed Opuscoli
scelte, 2 vol. *half bound*   *Brusselles*, 1841

926 Ademollo (A.) Marietta de' Ricci, 8 vol. *half morocco, in
case*   *Firenze*, 1840

927 Possevini (G. B.) Dialogo dell' Honore, *Vinegia*, 1563—
Libro delle Cose pertinenti all' Honore, *ivi*, 1562, in
one vol.—Paris de Puteo, Duello, *ivi*, 1525—Cittadini
(C.) delle Armi Gentilizie, *half morocco, Lucca*, 1741 (3)

928 Boetio della Consolatione de la Filosofia tradotto da C.
Bartoli, *Fiorenza, L. Torrentino,* 1551—Luciano dilette-
voli Dialogi, Narrationi e facete Epistole, *woodcuts,*
Vinegia, 1543 ; with Orosio tradotto per G. Guerini,
s. a. in the volume (2)

929 Giovio (P.) Vita di Consalvo Ferrando di Cordova detto
il Gran Capitano, *Fiorenza, L. Torrentino,* 1550—Vita
di Ferrando Davalo Marchese di Pescara, *ivi,* 1551 (2)

930 Porta (G.-B.) Miracoli dalla Natura e L. Lennio Secreti
Miracoli di Natura, 2 vol. in 1, *ruled, vol. II wants*
title, Venetia, 1560 — Lennio (L.) Occulti Miracoli,
ivi, 1567 (2)

931 Malatesta (G.) della nuova Poesia overo delle Difese del
Furioso Dialogo, *morocco, g. e.* *Verona,* 1589

932 Meli (G.) Poesie Siciliane, 4 vol. in 2, *portrait and cuts,*
half calf, Palermo, 1814 — Capassi (N.) Sonetti in
Dialetto Napoletano, *Napoli,* 1810—Carini (A. D. di)
Lu Vivu Mortu, *Palermo,* 1783—Piccinni (D.) Poesie
Italiane e in Dialetto Napoletano, *Napoli,* 1827 (5)

933 Cavalli (G. G.) Çittara Zeneise, *Genova,* 1745—Franchi
(S. de) Ro Chittarin, *Zena,* 1772 ; *in the Genoese*
Dialect (2)

934 Lotti (L.) Ch'n'ha' cervel hapa Gamb, *plates, Parma,* 1685
—Dialoghi, *frontispiece, Milano,* 1704 ; *in the Bolognese*
Dialect *in one vol.*

935 Rime di Magagno, Menon e Begotto in Lingua Rustica
Padouana, 3 vol. in 1, *scarce* *Venetia,* 1584

936 Cæsar, *ruled, russia, g. e.* *Lugd.* 1546

937 Westoniæ (Elisabethæ J.) Parthenicon, *calf* *Pragæ, s. a.*

938 Index Librorum prohibitorum *Mechliniæ,* 1860

939 Juris Quiritium vetustissimi Reliquias concinnabat E.
Thomson, *scarce* *Aeræ,* 1831

940 Tasse (T.) L'Aminte en Vers François (avec le Texte) en
Regard) *plates by Decker, vellum*
La Haye (Elzevier) 1681

941 Taxe de la Chancellerie Romaine ou la Banque du Pape,
old morocco, g. e. *Rome,* 1744

942 Menagiana, 4 vol. *with the cancelled leaves* (E iiii *and* v *in*
vol. III supplied in Manuscript) calf, g. e. *Paris,* 1720

943 Hopton (A.) Concordancy of Yeares, black letter, 1615—
Logarithmic Tables in Arabic, *scarce, Constantinople,*
circa 1840—Cooke (C. N.) American System of Book
Keeping, *Calcutta,* 1840 (3)

944 Walpole (Horace) Postscript to the Royal and Noble Authors. *Transcript of the rare Edition printed at Straw-*
berry Hill, 1786, engraved frontispiece, red morocco

945 Ritson (J.) Northern Garlands, *uncut,* 1810—Percy (Bp.
T.) Five Pieces of Runic Poetry, *calf,* 1763 (2)

946 Carmeni (F.) Nissena, an excellent new Romance, *with autograph of George Colt (see MS. note)* 1653
947 Johnson (S.) Julian the Apostate, *calf gilt, burnt by the Hangman, and Author fined 100 Marks* 1682
948 Hone (W.) House that Jack built, Man in the Moon, and Christmas Carol, *coloured cuts by G. Cruikshank, half morocco* 1819-20
949 Suffolk Garland *Ipswich*, 1818
950 Phillips (Sir R.) Mornings Walk from London to Kew, *half calf extra, uncut, top edges gilt* 1820
951 Bartell (E.) Cromer, *view, Holt*, 1800—Rye (W.) History of Cubitt Family, *Norwich*, 1873—Blenheim Guide, *Oxford*, 1803 (3)
952 Le Comte (L.) China, *plates*, 1737—Kidd (S.) China, *plates*, 1841—Lindsay and Gutzlaff's Report on a Voyage to China, 1834—Gutzlaff (C.) Three Voyages to China, *portrait, map and plates*, 1834—Arrowsmith's Map of Yang-Tsze-Kiang, *mounted on cloth, 3 copies*—Tarrant (W.) Hong Kong Government Ordinances, *officially marked "Incomplete Copy," Hong Kong*, 1850 (8)
953 Huggins (W.) Sketches in India, 1824—Buist (G.) Annals of India for 1848, *Bombay*, 1849—Letter from a Lady at Madras, 1743—Jackson (Sir C.) Vindication of the Marquis of Dalhousie's Indian Administration, 1865—Glen (W.) Tour from Astrachan to Karass, 1823; and 3 others (8)
954 Greaves (J.) Miscellaneous Works, 2 vol. *plates*, 1737—Illustrations of Egyptian Antiquities, *plates, Bath*, 1822—Wilkinson (Sir J. G.) Plates to Second Series of Ancient Egyptians, *wants plate 30 A, sold with all faults*, 1841—Gliddon (G. R.) Otia Ægyptiaca, 1849—Weijers (H. E.) over Job Ludolf, *Leyden*, 1838 (6)
955 Hodgson (B. H.) Pre-eminence of the Vernaculars (on Indian Education) *4 copies* *Serampore*, 1847
956 Jones (F.) Notes on Nineveh, *3 copies* 1855
957 Hamilton (W.) East-India Gazetteer, 2 vol. *maps, calf extra* 1828
958 Hamilton (W.) East-India Gazetteer, SECOND EDITION, 2 vol. *maps* *n. d.*
959 Cooper (F.) Crisis in the Punjaub, *map, 2 copies* 1858
960 Impey (E. B.) Memoirs of Sir E. Impey, *portrait, half calf gilt*, 1846—Maitre de La Tour (M.) History of Hyder Shah, 1848—Relation de Dourry Efendy, *Paris*, 1810 (3)
961 Indian Records between British Government and the Nawabs Nazim, *photograph*, 1876—Thomason's Despatches, vol. I, *Calcutta*, 1856—Selections from Government Records, North Western Provinces, *Alahabad*, 1864—Records of Andaman Islands, *Calcutta*, 1859 (4)

962 Weston (S.) Episodes of the Shah Nameh, in English
 Verse, 1815—Chinese Chronicle, 1820, with Fan-Hy-
 Chew, in Chinese and English, 1814; and Chinese
 Character, 1812, in the Volume, *morocco*—Ly Tang and
 Conquest of the Miao-Tse, 2 vol. *with S. Weston's auto-
 graph additions, morocco*, 1809-10—Moral Aphorisms,
 1805—Persian Distichs, 1814; with Remains of Arabic
 in Spanish and Portuguese, 1810, in the Volume—
 Persian Recreations, *portrait of Sir R. Shirley*, 1812—
 Specimens of Picturesque Poetry in Chinese, 2 *copies* (8)

963 Sady's Gulistan in Persian, 1809—Khanikof (N. de) sur
 Khâcâni Poëte Persan du XIIᵉ Siècle, *Paris*, 1865—
 Golshan-i-Sibyan, *Calcutta*, 1855—Turkish Proverbs,
 Venice, 1844 (4)

964 Jones (Siv W.) Poems 1777

965 Aucher (P.) Armenian and English Grammar (the English
 by Lord Byron) *Venice*, 1819

966 Lassen (C.) und N. L. Westergaard über Keilinschriften,
 Bonn, 1845 — Lassen (C.) Altpersische Keil-In-
 schriften, *ib.* 1836—Dietrich (F. E. C.) Zwei Sidonische
 Inschriften, *Marburg*, 1855—Osiander (E.) Himjar
 Alterthumskunde, *Leipzig*, 1864 — Movers (F. C.)
 Punischen Texte im Plautus erklärt, *Breslau*, 1845 (5)

967 Mutanabbi und Seifuddaula aus der Edelperle des Tsaâlibi
 dargestellt von F. Dietrici, *Leipzig*, 1847—Garcin de
 Tassy (M.) sur le Langage des Oiseaux, *Paris*, 1856;
 and 2 others by Garcin de Tassy (4)

968 Caspari (C. P.) Grammatica, *Lipsiæ*, 1848; with C. Rien
 de Abdul-Alae Vita et Carminibus, *Bonæ*, 1843—
 Bibliothecæ Orientalis, part I, *Lipsiæ*, 1840, in the
 Volume, *half calf*—Caussin de Perceval (A. P.) Grammaire Arabe vulgaire, *Paris*, 1833—Ewald (G. H. A.)
 de Metris Carminum Arabicorum, *Brunsvigæ*, 1825—
 Jahn (J.) Arabische Chrestomathie, *Wien*, 1802 (4)

969 Sacy (A. I. Silvestre de) Grammaire Arabe, 2 vol. *Paris*,
 1810 — Chrestomathie Arabe, 3 vol. *ib.* 1806, *calf
 extra* 5 *vol.*

970 Humbert (J.) Arabica Analecta inedita, *Paris*, 1838—
 Historia Califatus Al-Motacimi, *Lugd. Bat.* 1849; and
 4 others (6)

971 Wüstenfels (F.) Geschichte der Arabischen Ærzte und
 Naturforscher *Göttingen*, 1840

972 Zanolini (A.) Grammatica Syriaca, *Patavii*, 1742—Cowper
 (B. H.) Syriac Miscellanies, 1861—Nork (F.) Die
 Götter Syriens, *Stuttgart*, 1842—Lipsius (R. A.) über
 die Æchtheit der Syrischen Recension der Ignatiani-
 schen Briefe, *Gotha*, 1856 (4)

973 Haughton (Sir G. C.) on Vedanta Philosophy, *calf gilt,*
     1835—Ram Das Sen on Modern Buddhistic Researches,
     privately printed, Calcutta, 1874—Browne (J. C.) Indian
     Infanticide, 1857   (3)

974 Pauli (C. W. H.) Analecta Hebraica, *Oxford,* 1839—Je-
     huda Ben Koreisch (R.) de Studii Targum Utilitate
     Heb. *Paris,* 1857—De Rossi (J. B.) Lexicon Hebraicum
     Selectum, *Parmæ,* 1805—Seder Olam Rabba, translated
     by J. Williams, 1861—Buxtorfii (J.) Lexicon Hebrai-
     cum et Chaldaicum, 1646 ; and 2 other Hebrew Works

975 Laounds (I.) Lexicon Hebraico-Neohellenicum
                                             Melite, 1842

976 Salisbury (R. A.) Genera of Plants, a Fragment con-
     taining Part of Liriogamæ, 2 *copies*   1866

977 Palmer (W.) on Orthodox or Eastern-Catholic Com-
     munion   1853

978 Book of Common Prayer for the Protestant Episcopal
     Church in the United States of America, *calf extra*
                                             New York, 1844

979 Brooke (R.) Liverpool, *plates, a few additional*
                                             Liverpool, 1853

980 Gœthe (J. W. von) Werke, 2 vol. *half morocco*
                                             Stuttgart, 1845-46

981 Hoffmann (E. T. W.) Sämmtliche Werke, *portrait, half
     morocco*   *Paris,* 1841

982 Micali (G.) Storia degli antichi Popoli Italiani, 3 vol.
                                             Firenze, 1832

983 Milano e il suo Territorio, 2 vol. *plates*   *Milano,* 1844

984 Descrizione di Genova e del Genovesato, 3 vol. *plates*
                                             Genova, 1846

985 Dante Alighieri, Divina Commedia e Rime. Manoscritta da
     Boccaccio, 4 vol. *half morocco*   *Roveta,* 1820

986 Dante Alighieri, Commedia col Comento di N. Tommaseo,
     3 vol. *half russia*   *Venezia,* 1837

987 Dante Alighieri, Divina Commedia, 2 vol. *portrait, half
     russia*   *Firenze,* 1837

988 Tasso (T.) Jerusalem delivered, translated by J. H. Wif-
     fen, vol. I, *portrait and woodcuts,* 1824—Castelli's His-
     torical Prints to Tasso, *portraits and plates, n. d.*   (2)

989 Attila Flagellum Dei Poemetto in ottava Rima, *half calf,
     uncut, top edge gilt*   *Pisa,* 1864

990 Guerino detto il Meschino, *plates, a Prose Romance*
                                             Milano, 1841

991 Cuvier (Baron) Animal Kingdom, with additional Descrip-
     tions by E. Griffith and others, with Classified Index
     and Synopsis, 16 vol. LARGE PAPER, *coloured plates*
                                             1827-35

992 Timperley (C. H.) Typographical Dictionary, No. I to
XXVII (wanting No. V)—Hughes (W.) Scripture
Atlas, 1840—Key to Political Sketches of H. B.—
Nares (R.) Glossary, part X, 1858 ; and others, *a parcel*

993 Catalogues. London Library, 2 vol. 1847-52—Payne and
Foss, 1837 and 1840—T. Payne, 1766—Hotten (J. C.)
Handbook to Topography ; and others (24)

994 Catalogues. Sale, Booksellers, &c. *many scarce and valuable for reference (some priced)* *a large parcel*

995 Biblia Hebraica, *Amst.* 1639 —Vitringa (C.) Typus
Theologiæ practicæ *Franeq.* 1716—Ostervald (J. F.)
Traité contre l' Impurité, *Amst.* 1707—Pseaumes en
Rime par C. Marot et T. de Beze, *with music, La Haye,*
1731—Elis (J.) Articulorum XXXIX Defensio. Acce-
dunt Articuli Lambethani, *Amst.* 1700

996 Goodwin (T.) Returns of Prayers, 1636—Mackenzie
(Sir G.) Moral Essay preferring Solitude to public Em-
ployment, 1685—Magna Charta cum Statutis, 1618 (3)

997 Bridges (C.) Christian Ministry, 1830—Speculum Episcopi, 1849—Keith (A.) on Prophecy, *plates, Edinb.* 1835
—Bailey (H. I.) Liturgy compared with the Bible,
1839—Doddridge (P.) Rise and Progress of Religion
in the Soul, *portrait, Glasgow,* 1825 (5)

998 Wiseman (N. Cardinal) Lectures on the Catholic Church,
2 vol. 1836—Secreta Monita Societatis Jesu, in Latin
and English, 1723—Bellarmine (R. Cardinal) Short
Christian Doctrine in Italian and English, *Rome,* 1836
—Bird (C. S.) Strictures on Wilberforce's Works on
the Incarnation and Eucharist, 1854 (5)

999 Evelyn (J.) Life of Mrs. Godolphin, *portrait,* 1848—
Sherer (M.) Life of Duke of Wellington, vol. I, 1830—
Field (J.) Life of John Howard, *portrait,* 1850 (3)

1000 Theological Library, viz.: Le Bas (C. W.) Lives of
Wiclif, Archbp. Cranmer and Bp. Jewel, 4 vol. 1832-35—
Smedley (E.) History of the Reformed Religion in France,
3 vol. 1832-34—Shuttleworth (Bp. P. N.) on Revelation, 1832—Evans (R. W.) Scripture Biography and
Biography of the Early Church, Second Series, 2 vol.
1834-39—Russell (M.) History of the Church in Scotland, 2 vol. 1834, *portraits* 12 *vol.*

1001 Soames (H.) Anglo-Saxon Church and Elizabethan Religious History, 2 vol. 1838-39

1002 Riddle (J. E.) Ecclesiastical Chronology 1840

1003 Fleury (Abbé) Ecclesiastical History (381-400) by J. H.
Newman *Oxford,* 1842

1004 Mosheim (J. L.) Ecclesiastical History, 6 vol. *russia
extra* 1826

1005 Waddington (G.) History of the Church to the Reformation   1833
1006 Strype (L.) Ecclesiastical Memorials of the Reformation
under Henry VIII, Edward VI, and Mary I, 7 vol. 1816
1007 Hunter (H.) Sacred Biography, 5 vol.   1820
1008 Hay (J.) Divinity Lectures, 3 vol.   *Camb.* 1796-7
1009 Testament (New) in Greek, with English Notes by S. T.
Bloomfield, 2 vol.   1839
1010 Townsend (G.) Old and New Testament, arranged in
historical and chronological order, 4 vol.   1821-5
1011 Mant (Bp. R.) Scriptural Narratives of Our Lord's Life
and Ministry. *Oxford*, 1830—Book of Common Prayer,
with Notes by Bp. R. Mant, 2 vol. *ib.* 1824   (3)
1012 Shepherd (J.) on the Book of Common Prayer, 2 vol. 1817
1013 Jay (W.) Morning Exercises, 2 vol. *half calf*   1839
1014 Davenant (Bp. J.) on the Colossians, translated by J.
Allport, 2 vol. *portrait, Birm.* 1831-32—Newton (Sir I.)
on the Prophecies of Daniel, 1831—Stuart (M.) on
Hebrews, 1834—Oliver (P.) Scripture Lexicon, *Oxford*,
1810   (5)
1015 Formularies of Faith put forth by Authority during the
Reign of Henry VIII (edited by C. Lloyd) *Oxf.* 1825
1016 Cardwell (E.) Two Books of Common Prayer of Edward VI
compared, *Oxford*, 1838—Documentary Annals of the
Reformed Church of England, with Notes, 2 vol. *ib.* 1839
—Synodalia, with Notes, 2 vol. *ib.* 1842   *5 vol.*
1017 Palmer (W.) Origines Liturgicæ, 2 vol.   *Oxford*, 1832
1018 Nixon (Bp. F. R.) on the Church Catechism   1846
1019 Potter (Archbp. J.) on Church-Government, 1711—
Whiston (W.) Six Dissertations, 1734—Cove (M.) on
Church-Revenues, 1816   (3)
1020 Keble (J.) Christian Year, *second edition* *Oxford*, 1827
1021 Davison (J.) Remains and Occasional Publications
Oxford, 1841
1022 Grant (A.) The Nestorians, *map, half calf gilt*   1841
1023 Mendham (J.) Literary Policy of the Church of Rome,
1830—Hereford Discussion between Rev. J. Venn and
Rev. J. Waterworth, *Hereford*, 1844   (2)
1024 Faber (G. S.) Difficulties of Romanism   1830
1025 Horne (T. H.) Introduction to the Critical Study and
Knowledge of the Holy Scriptures, 4 vol. *maps and facsimiles*   1834
1026 Leighton (Archbp. R.) Works, with Life by Rev. J. N.
Pearson, 4 vol. *portrait*   1830
1027 Baxter (R.) Practical Works, with Life by Rev. W. Orme,
23 vol. *portrait*   1830
1028 Howe (J.) Works, 7 vol. *portraits, vol. I wants title, &c.
sold with all faults, half calf*   1811-16

1029 Lardner (N.) Works, with Life by A. Kippis, 10 vol. 1834
1030 Library of the Fathers, viz.: St. John Chrysostom's
Homilies on Corinthians, Romans, and on the Statues,
4 vol. *Oxford*, 1839-42 — St. Cyril's Catechetical Lectures *ib.* 1838—St. Athanasius's Select Treatises, *ib.*
1842—St. Augustine's Confessions, *ib.* 1838—Tertul-
lian's Apologetic and Practical Treatises, *ib.* 1842   (8)
1031 Hall (R.) Works, 6 vol. *portrait*   1831-32
1032 Bridgewater Treatises, by T. Chalmers, 2 vol. 1833—W.
Whewell, 1833—Sir C. Bell, 1833—W. Buckland, 2 vol.
1836—W. Kirby, 2 vol. 1835, and W. Prout, 1834 9 *vol.*
1033 Nares (R.) on the Prophecies, 1805—Discourses and Sermons, 2 vol. 1794-1825, *calf gilt*   3 *vol.*
1034 Smith (J. Pye) on the Messiah, 3 vol. 1829—On the
Sacrifice of Christ, 1813, and other Tracts in the vol. (4)
1035 Horsley (S.) Biblical Criticism, 4 vol. 1820—Nine Sermons and Dissertations on the Prophecies, 1815 5 *vol.*
1036 Arnold (T.) Sermons on Christian Life, 1841—Hare (J.
C.) Victory of Faith, and other Sermons, 1840—Mas-
sillon (Bp. P.) Charges, 1805—Nares (R.) Discourses
and Sermons, 2 vol. *half calf gilt*, 1794-1825—Barrow
(I.) Eighteen Sermons, 1849   (6)
1037 Enfield (W.) Sermons, 3 vol. *portrait*, *calf*, 1798—Sermons by various Authors, in 5 vol. *half calf, v. y.*   (8)
1038 Routh (M. J.) Scriptorum Ecclesiasticorum Opuscula, Gr.
et Lat. 2 vol.   *Oxon.* 1840
1039 Goode (W.) Divine Rule of Faith and Practice, 3 vol. 1853
1040 Graves (R.) on the Pentateuch, *Dublin*, 1831—Lowman
(M.) on the Hebrew Ritual, *half calf gilt*, 1816—Bridges
(C.) Christian Ministry, 1835   (3)
1041 Whately (Abp. R.) on Difficulties in St. Paul's Writings,
1828—Rhetoric, 1836   (2)
1042 Jebb (Bp. J.) Sacred Literature, 1828—Thirty Years'
Correspondence with A. Knox, 2 vol. 1834   (3)
1043 Burnet (Bp. G.) History of his own Time, 4 vol. *portrait*,
calf   1818
1044 Lardner Cabinet Cyclopædia, 43 vol.   1829-35
1045 Whewell (W.) on English University Education, 1837—
Abercrombie (J.) on the Intellectual Powers, *Edinb.*
1835—Sewell (W.) Introduction to the Dialogues of
Plato, 1841—Somerville (Mrs.) on the Connexion of the
Physical Sciences, 1834   (4)
1046 Lyell (Sir C.) Elements of Geology, 1838—Principles of
Geology, 4 vol. 1834, *plates*   5 *vol.*
1047 Darwin (R. W.) Principia Botanica, *Newark*, 1787—
Rousseau (J. J.) Plantes coloriées, *coloured plates, Par.*
1789—Donn (J.) Hortus Cantabrigiensis, *Camb.* 1812—
Dennis (J.) Landscape Gardener, *plates*, 1835   (4)

1048 Withering (W.) Systematic Arrangement of British
Plants, 4 vol. *plates* *Birm.* 1812
1049 Higgins (W. M.) Mosaic and Mineral Geologies, 1832—
Wood (N.) Ornithologists' Text-Book, 1836—Hannam
(J.) on Waste Manures, 1844 (3)
1050 Samouelle (G.) Entomologist's useful Compendium,
plates 1819
1051 Trollope (Mrs.) Belgium and Western Germany, 2 vol.
1834—Hartley (J.) Researches in Greece and the Levant,
1831—Downes (J.) Letters from Mecklenburg and
Holstein, 1822 (4)
1052 Whewell (W.) on German Churches, *plates, Camb.* 1842
—Markland (J. H.) on English Churches, *plates, Oxford,*
1842 (2)
1053 Morier (J.) Zohrab the Hostage, 3 vol. 1833—Ayesha
the Maid of Kars, 3 vol. 1834 (6)
1054 Morton (Hon. Mrs. Erskine) The Gossip, 3 vol. 1852—
Emma, 3 vol. 1773—Sandford and Merton, 3 vol. *plates
by Stothard,* 1795 (9)
1055 Shakespeare (W.) Works, with Notes by L. Theobald,
8 vol. *portrait and plates* 1773
1056 Gay (J.) Poems, 2 vol. *plates,* 1753—Modern Manners,
frontispiece, 1782—Somervile (W.) Hobbinol and the
Chase, *plates,* 1757, with other Poems in the vol. (4)
1057 Cowper (W.) Task, *plates by Westall,* 1817—Poetry of
the Anti-Jacobin, 1807—Stuart (J.) Poems, *Belfast,*
1811— Jesse (J. H.) London, 1847 (4)
1058 Stow (J.) Survey of London, edited by W. J. Thoms, 1842
1059 Edmondson (J.) Present Peerages, *plates of arms* 1785
1060 Collet (S. *i. e.* J. S. Byerley) Relics of Literature, *facsimiles of autographs, half calf gilt* 1823
1061 Siddons (H.) on Gesture and Action, *plates* 1807
1062 Demosthenis et Æschinis Opera Græce, 2 vol. 1824—
Sophoclis Tragœdiæ Græce, *Oxon.* 1834—Aristotelis
Politica et Œconomica, Gr. et Lat. 2 vol. *ib.* 1810 (5)
1063 Theatre of the Greeks, *Camb.* 1820—Valpy (F. E. J.)
Latin Etymological Dictionary, *calf extra,* 1828—Porti
(M. A.) Lexicon Ionicum, *Oxon.* 1818 (3)
1064 Nizolii (M.) Lexicon Ciceronianum, 3 vol. 1820
1065 Quarterly Review, from the commencement in 1809 to
October 1844 inclusive, with Indexes, 74 vol. *half calf*
(*wanting vol. XLIV*) 1809-44
1066 Quarterly Review, No. 88, 90, 96 to 113, 115 to 118,
121, 123 to 133, 135, 136, 138 to 140, 147, 150, 154,
156 to 158, 161 to 163, and 168, together 52 Nos. 1831-49
1067 Mackintosh (Sir J.) on Ethical Philosophy, *Edinb.* 1836
1068 Gorton (J.) Topographical Dictionary of Great Britain
and Ireland, 3 vol. *maps* 1833

1069 Hutton (C.) Mathematical Tables, 1801—Bridge (B.)
Algebra, 1840 (2)

1070 Robertson (W.) Works, with Life by D. Stewart, viz. :
History of Scotland, 3 vol. *portrait*, 1809—History of
Charles V, 4 vol. *portraits and plates*, 1809—History of
America, 4 vol. *maps*, 1808—Historical Disquisition on
India, 1809, *russia extra* 12 *vol.*

1071 Robertson (W.) Works, 8 vol. *portrait* *Oxford*, 1825

1072 Roberts (Emma) Memoirs of the Rival Houses of York
and Lancaster, 2 vol. *portrait, half calf* 1827

1073 Russell (W.) History of Modern Europe, with Continuation to 1802 by C. Coote, 6 vol. *old gilt calf* 1810

1074 Smyth (W.) Lectures on Modern History, 2 vol. 1841

1075 Foy (General) History of the War in the Peninsula,
2 vol. in 3, *portrait* 1827

1076 Bacon (Lord Chancellor) Works, with Life by Basil
Montagu, 16 vol. in 17, *portrait* 1825-34

1077 Dibdin (T. F.) Bibliotheca Spenceriana, 4 vol. *numerous
elegant facsimiles, uncut* 1814-15

1078 Church of England Magazine, 15 vol. *plates (wanting vol.
V, VIII, XII and XIV)* 1836-43

1079 Levi (L.) International Commercial Law, 2 vol. 1863

1080 Newton (C. T.) Travels and Discoveries in the Levant,
2 vol. *maps and plates* 1865

1081 Froude (J. A.) History of England, from the Fall of
Wolsey to the Defeat of the Spanish Armada, 12 vol.
morocco extra 1867-70

1082 McCulloch (J. R.) Geographical Dictionary, by F. Martin,
4 vol. *coloured maps, half calf gilt, m. e.* 1866

1083 Burke (Sir B.) Book of Orders of Knighthood, 500 *facsimile illustrations of the various Insignia, coloured by
hand* 1858

1084 Hall (Bp. J.) Works, by P. Wynter, 10 vol. *calf gilt,
m. e.* , *Oxford*, 1863

1085 Robinson (E.) Biblical Researches in Palestine, 3 vol.
maps and plans, calf, full gilt backs, m. e. 1867

1086 Ritter (C.) Geography of Palestine and the Sinaitic
Peninsula, by W. L. Gage, 4 vol. in 2, *map and cuts,
morocco gilt, g. e.* *Edinb.* 1866

1087 Percy (Bp. T.) Folio Manuscript: Ballads and Romances,
including Loose and Humorous Songs, edited by J. W.
Hales and F. J. Furnivall, 4 vol. *morocco antique* 1867

1088 HANSARD'S PARLIAMENTARY HISTORY AND DEBATES,
FROM THE COMMENCEMENT IN 1066 TO 1875, viz.
Parliamentary History, from 1066 to 1803, 36 vol.
1806-20—Parliamentary Debates. First Series, 1803
to 1820, 41 vol.—Second Series, 1820 to 1830, 25 vol.
—General Index, 1803-30—Third Series, with Con-

60

tinuation from 1830 to vol. 225, part 7, 1875 (*wanting numbers 24 and 30 of 1875*); together 320 vol. and 57 Nos. *from 1806 to 1835 (133 vol.) half russia, and from 1836 to 1873 in boards, the remainder in Nos.;* and 9 duplicate General Indexes from 1865 to 1873 (386)

1089 Smollett (T.) History of England, 15 vol. *portraits and plates, calf*   1758-61

1090 Wolcot (J.) Works of Peter Pindar, 5 vol. *portrait, half calf*   1812

1091 Ticozzi (S.) Dizionario dei Pittori, 2 vol. in 1, *half morocco*   *Milano*, 1818

QUARTO.

1092 ISMAIL IBN-MAKRI, UNWAN-AL-SHARAF. Treatises on Theology, Descendants of the Prophet, Prosody, &c. in Arabic, MANUSCRIPT, *having each page divided into seven columns, written alternately in red and black ink, in Oriental binding,* EXCESSIVELY RARE, IF NOT UNIQUE

**** A truly curious and very extraordinary work, which could only have been written in Arabic, and even in that language is so unique that the Author confidently offered to bestow his favorite wife on any man who should compose a similar one. The several columns contain distinct Treatises on Prosody, the Descendants of the Prophets, &c. if read perpendicularly, but if perused without paying any attention to the divisions it presents a perfect and elaborate Treatise on the Mahomedan Religion.

1093 Commentary wholly Biblical, 3 vol. *coloured maps, calf antique, r. e.*   *Bagster*

1094 Whitney (G.) Choice of Emblemes, and other Devises, a facsimile reprint of the 1586 edition, edited by H. Green, *with the numerous woodcuts of emblems, &c. morocco antique, g. e.*   1866

1095 Testament (New), *Longman's beautiful edition, printed within ornamental borders, &c. with engravings after Fra Angelico, Titian, Raphael and others, morocco extra, inlaid and full gilt sides, g. e.*   1865

1096 Shakespeare (W.) Comedies, Histories and Tragedies, reprint of the 1623 edition, *port. morocco antique* 1864

1097 BLANC (C.) HISTOIRE DES PEINTRES, de toutes les Ecoles, Française, 3 vol.—Hollandaise, 2 vol.—Flamande —Anglaise par M. W. Bürger—Vénitienne—Espagnole —Ombrienne et Romaine; together 10 vol. *several hundred fine engravings, half morocco, g. e. Paris,* 1863-71

1098 English Cyclopædia, Arts and Sciences, 8 vol. in 4, *illustrated, half russia, m. c.* *n. d.*
1099 Cohn's Hexaglot Bible, vol. I 1868
1100 Marcoy (P.) Journey across South America, half-vol. 2, half-vol. 3, *engravings* 1873
1101 Furnivall (F. J.) Early English Meals and Manners, LARGE PAPER, *plates* 1868
1102 Hardwicke's Science-Gossip, vol. 4, 5, 6, in 1 vol. *cuts, half calf* 1869-71
1103 Bible (Holy), *Camb.* 1673 — Bible, *Oxford*, 1754— Bythneri (V.) Lyra Prophetica Davidis Regis, 1679 ; and 1 other (4)
1104 Johnson (S.) English Dictionary, with numerous Additions by Rev. H. J. Todd, 5 vol. in 11 parts, *port.* 1818
1105 List of Illustrations to the Catalogue of the Society of British Artists in the possession of Mr. Jupp, *unbound* 13 *copies*
1106 The same, *printed on vellum* 2 *copies*
1107 Foxi (J.) de Christo crucifixo Concio 1571
1108 Liturgies. Form of Common Prayer for the late Naval Victory, 1666 — Charles II, Declaration concerning Treasonable Conspiracy, 1683 — Form of Prayer for Discovery of the late Conspiracy, 1683 — Form for Victories over Rebels, 1685—Form for 29 April, 1691, black letter (5)
1109 Psalterium Beati Brunonis *Noremb.* 1497
1110 Babington (Bp. G.) Notes on Genesis, black letter, 1596 — Burton (H.) Tryal of Private Devotion, 1628 — Speculum Crape-Gownorum, part II, 1682—Weemse (J.) Pourtraiture of the Image of God in Man, 1627— Stillingfleet (Bp. E.) Unreasonableness of Separation, 1681 (5)
1111 Cardanus (H. C.) Comforte, translated by Thomas Bedingfield, black letter, *calf* *T. Marsh,* 1576
1112 Prisei (J.) Historiæ Britannicæ Defensio et Monæ Insula Descriptio *H. Binneman,* 1573
1113 Wandering-Jew telling Fortunes to English-men, *woodcut, several leaves mended, calf gilt* 1640
1114 Carrillo (M.) Explicacion de la Bula de los Difuntos con Apologia, 2 vol. in 1, *scarce* *Alcala,* 1615
1115 Buch von dem Leben und Sitten der Heynischen Maister, black letter, *woodcut capitals, rare* *Augspurg, A. Sorg,* 1490
1116 Luther (M.) Book of Vagabonds and Beggars, with Vocabulary of their Language, translated by J. C. Hotten, *half morocco, top edge gilt* 1860
1117 Ariosto (L.) Orlando Furioso, *woodcuts* *Venetia,* 1619

1118 Ariosto (L.) Cinque Canti iquali segvono la Materia del
Furioso, *woodcuts, rare*   *Pesaro*, 1556
1119 Tasso (T.) il Goffredo travestito alla Rustica Bergamasca
da C. Assonica (col Testo)   *Venetia*, 1670
1120 Filicaia (V. da) Poesie Toscane   *Firenze*, 1707
1121 Dante Alighieri, La Divina Commedia con Note, *plates,
half bound*   *Bologna*, 1826
1122 Boiardo Conte di Scandiano (M. M.) Sonetti e Canzone,
LARGE PAPER (*only 50 copies printed*)   *Milano*, 1845
1123 Manzoni (A.) Opere varie, *plates, half russia*   *ib.* 1845
1124 Ferrari (G.) Notizie storiche della Lega tra l'Imperatore
Carlo VI e la Republica di Venezia   *Venezia*, 1723
1125 Comines (F. di) Memorie, *half bound, uncut Venetia*, 1640
1126 Colucci (G.) Treja antica Città Picena oggi Montecchio
illustrata   *Macerata*, 1780
1127 Bugni (S.) Lectures on Italy and the Italians, MANU-
SCRIPT   1835
1128 Storia de' SS. Barlaam e Giosaffatte   *Roma*, 1734
1129 Ceoldo (P.) Albero della Famiglia Papafava, *Venezia*,
1801—Armauni (V.) della Famiglia Capizucchi, *portrait
and plates, Roma*, 1668   (2)
1130 Patriarchi (G.) Vocabolario Veneziano e Padovano, *half
morocco, uncut, top edge gilt*   *Padova*, 1821
1131 Baldassini (G.) Memorie istoriche di Jesi   *Jesi*, 1765
1132 Fiorentini (F. M.) Memorie della Gran Contessa Matilda
con Note da G. D. Mansi, 2 vol. *uncut*   *Lucca*, 1756
1133 Rosmini (Cav. C. de') Vita di G. J. Trivulzio detto il
Magno, 2 vol. *half bound, uncut*   *Milano*, 1815
1134 Vitale (F. A.) Storia diplomatica de' Senatori di Roma,
2 vol.   *Roma*, 1791
1135 Casano (A.) del Sotterraneo della Chièsa Cattedrale di
Palermo   *Palermo*, 1849
1136 Frisi (A. F.) Memorie della Chièsa Monzese, 3 parts in 1,
plates, half calf gilt   *Milano*, 1774-77
1137 Bembi (P. Cardinalis) Historia Veneta   *Lutetiæ*, 1551
1138 Sestini (D.) Viaggio da Costantinopoli a Bassora, *plates,
uncut*   *Yverdun*, 1786
1139 ORIENTAL LITERATURE. A Collection of 80 various
Works in the Arabic, Persian, Turkish, Hindustani,
and other Dialects of the East   (80)
1140 Rosenmülleri (E. F. C.) Institutiones ad Fundamenta
Linguæ Arabicæ. Accedunt Sententiæ et Narrationes
Arabicæ una cum Glossario Arabico-Latino, *Lipsiæ*,
1818—Seaman (G.) Grammatica Turcica, *Oxon.* 1670—
Synopsis Propositorum Sapientiæ Arabum Philosopho-
rum, Arab. et Lat. *Paris*, 1641   (3)
1141 Hyde (T.) Syntagma Dissertationum et Opuscula inedita
cum Vita, 2 vol. *portrait*   *Oxon.* 1767

1142 Rozet us Safa, vol. VI—Sadi Gulistan—Behari Dunish
  —Akhlak Mohsum, by Hussan Vaez Cashifi; and 6
  other Oriental Manuscripts (9)
1143 Abravanel (Rabbi I.) Mashmia Veshuah — Ejusdem
  Commentarii in Danielem et de Mundi Innovatione,
  2 vol. in 1, *vellum*—Khalvka de Rabbanan, *printed on
  blue paper;* and 3 others, Hebrew (6)
1144 Maimonidis (R. Mosis) Porta Mosis, Heb. et Lat. *Oxon.*
  1655—Lipmanni (Rabbi) Nizachon, Heb. et Lat. *Norib.*
  1644—Abarbanel (R. Ishak) Commentarius super
  Danielem, Heb. 1647—Cans (D.) Naim Verechmad,
  Heb. 1743—Schickardi (W.) Jus Regium Hebræorum,
  Lipsiæ, 1674; with Wolfii (J. C.) Notitia Karæorum,
  Hamb. 1721, in the volume (5)
1145 Nicolay (N. de) Reysen in Turckeyen, black letter, *plates
  of Costume from designs by Titian, vellum*
                    Antwerpen, 1576
1146 Map of Russia, *mounted on cloth, in case*—French Retreat
  from Moscow, 1813; and 1 other (3)
1147 Seneca's First Book of Clemency, in Verse, *scarce* 1653
1148 Collier (J. P.) Miscellaneous Tracts, part I and II
  (Perimedes by R. Greene, and Strange Newes by T.
  Nashe), *rare* *n. d.* (1865)
1149 Motherwell (W.) Minstrelsy, *half morocco, uncut, top
  edge gilt* *Paisley,* 1873
1150 Rennell (J.) Memoir of a Map of Hindoostan, *maps,
  russia, g. e. back broken* 1793
1151 Cochran-Patrick (R. W.) Early Records relating to
  Mining in Scotland, *facsimiles of autographs, half morocco, uncut, top edge gilt* *Edinb.* 1878
1152 Robinson (J. B.) Derbyshire Gatherings, *portraits of
  eminent Natives and eccentric Characters, Views, Facsimiles of Autographs, &c. cloth, g. e.* *Derby,* 1866
1153 Hilpert (J. L.) English-German Dictionary, 2 vol. in 1,
  half bound *Carlsruhe,* 1828-31
1154 Gigli (G.) Vocabolario Cateriniano, *portrait, uncut*
                    Manilla, s. a.
1155 Dizionario della Lingua Italiana (da P. Costa, F.
  Cardinali e F. Orioli), 7 vol. in 3, *half calf*
                    Bologna, 1819-26
1156 Hall (Bp. J.) on English Episcopacie, 1640—Burnet
  (Bp. G.) Pastoral Cure and Sermons, in 1 vol. 1692-
  1714—Stillingfleet (Bp. E.) Origines Sacræ, 1680 (3)
1157 Bible (English), by R. B. Blackader 1853
1158 Wall (W.) History of Infant Baptism, 1707—Wollaston
  (W.) Religion of Nature, *portrait,* 1738—Ogilvie (J.)
  Poems, *vignettes,* 1762 (3)

1159 Morell (T.) Lexicon Græco-Prosodiacum auctum ab E.
Maltby, *portraits, calf*, 1824—Hederici (B.) Græcum
Lexicon Manuale, 1790—Parkhurst (J.) Greek and
English Lexicon, 1769 (3)

1160 Adams (G.) Essays on the Microscope, with Additions
by F. Kanmacher, *plates* 1798

1161 Hooke (N.) Roman History, vol. I to III, *maps and
plates* 1738-64

1162 Anderson (W.) History of France, 5 vol. 1769-82

1163 ENCYCLOPÆDIA BRITANNICA, *8th edition*, 22 vol. and
Dissertation 6, *maps and plates* *Edinb.* 1856

1164 Addison (J.) Works, 4 vol. *portrait and plates by Hay-
man, binding broken* *Baskerville*, 1761

1165 Letter Copying Book, with Index ; and others (7)

1166 Desgranges (M.) Grammaire Sanscrit-Française, 2 vol.
Paris, 1845-47

1167 Desgranges.   The same, 2 copies
1168 Desgranges.   The same, 3 copies
1169 Desgranges.   The same, 4 copies
1170 Desgranges.   The same, 4 copies
1171 Desgranges.   The same, 5 copies
1172 Desgranges.   The same, 6 copies
1173 Desgranges.   The same, 6 copies
1174 Desgranges.   The same, 6 copies
1175 Desgranges.   The same, 6 copies
1176 Desgranges.   The same, 6 copies
1177 Desgranges.   The same, 6 copies
1178 Desgranges.   The same, 6 copies
1179 Desgranges.   The same, 6 copies
1180 Desgranges.   The same, 6 copies
1181 Desgranges.   The same, 6 copies
1182 Desgranges.   The same, 6 copies
1183 Desgranges.   The same, 6 copies
1184 Desgranges.   The same, 6 copies

AUTOGRAPH LETTERS.

1185 Cobden (Richard) eminent Politician
A. L. s.   To John Moss, dated *Dec. 27th*, 1845
An interesting letter, in which the following passage
occurs : " Peel charged me with a desire to procure his
assassination, and he has not retracted or explained."
His remarks follow (1)

1186 Russell (Earl)
Two A. L. s.   To John Moss, dated *August 1st*, 1855,
and March 26th, 1856, respectively
"Trusts that the cause of civil and religious freedom will
continue to make progress." (2)

1187 Wellington (Duke of)
    Two Autograph Notes in the third person, to Mr. Moss,
      dated 1846   (2)

1188 Montgomery (J.) Poet
    Two Notes to Mr. Moss, enclosing a Poem in four
      verses, entitled "The Christian Graces," dated *Feby.*
      5th, 1847   (2)

1189 Wharncliffe (Lord) A. L. s. to J. Moss, dated *Nov.*
      1849—Newcastle (Duke of) dated *29th Decr.* 1851,
      both on political subjects   (2)

1190 Whateley (Acbp.) to the same in the third person, Sir
      Robert Peel, Lord Morpeth, &c.   (6)

1191 Faraday (Michael) Philosopher
    A. L. s. to the same, dated *Feby.* 19*th*, 1845, on the
      subject of professional analysis   (1)

FOLIO.

1192 Music. Handel's Oratorios, Concertos, &c. in Score
                                               19 vol.

1193 Music. Gibbons (O.) First Set of Madrigals, by Sir
      G. Smart—Purcell (H.) Dido and Æneas—Byrd (W.)
      Mass for Five Voices, by E. F. Rimbault, *Musical*
      Antiquarian Society, 1841 ; &c.   (3)

1194 Music. Thomas (J.) Welsh Melodies, arranged for the
      Harp—Music for the Harp, and Harp and Piano Forte,
      5 vol.   (6)

1195 Music, principally for the P. F. &c.   *7 vol.*

1196 Music. Bickham (G.) Musical Entertainer, 2 vol. in 1,
      numerous engravings   *n. d.*

1197 Music for the Piano Forte, and Harp and P. F. *a parcel*

1198 Camden (W.) History of Queen Elizabeth, *imperfect*,
      1675—Buck (G.) History of Richard the Third, *por-*
      trait by Cross, 1647   (2)

1199 Newton (C. T.) and R. P. Pullan, Discoveries at Hali-
      carnassus, Cnidus and Branchidæ, 97 *large plates, some*
      in tints, with Text, 2 vol. 8*vo.* 1862   (3)

1200 Raccinet (M. A.) L'Ornement Polychrome, vol. I, 50 *fine*
      plates in gold and colours, half morocco   1871

1201 Bible (Sainte) 2 vol. *with the very numerous fine engra-*
      vings by G. Doré, ORIGINAL FRENCH EDITION, *morocco*
      extra, g. e. with joints   *Tours,* 1866

1202 Homeri Ilias per Laurentium Vallensem in Latinum Ser-
      monem traducta, *Brixiæ*, 1497—Homeri Odyssea G.
      Maxello alias Uebelin Interprete, *Argentoraci*, 1510—
      Guntheri Ligurini de Gestis Friderici I, Libri X, Car-
      mine heroico conscripti, *Augustæ*, 1507   *in 1 vol.*

1203 Ciceronis Tusculanæ Quæstiones, *Venetiis*, 1482—Cicero de Finibus, *ib.* (1480) *in 1 vol.*
1204 Dionysii Halicarnasei Antiquitates Romanæ Lappo Birago Interprete *Tarvisii*, 1480
1205 Johannes Chrysostomus super Mattheum et super Johannem, 2 vol. in 1, *stained, oak boards, covered in leather, with brass clasps* *Coloniæ*, 1487-86
1206 Malogranati Dialogus, *oak boards, covered in pigskin* *Anno* 1487
1207 Homeliarius Doctorum *Basileæ*, 1498
1208 Petri de Bergomo super omnia Opera Thomæ Aquinatis Tabula *Basileæ*, 1478
1209 Criniti (P.) Commentarii de honesta disciplina *Florentiæ, P. de Giunta,* 1504
1210 Plauti Comœdiæ *Mediolani,* 1490
1211 Rubei (H.) Historiæ Ravennatis *Venetiis, Aldus,* 1572
1212 Septimancensis (J.) Institutiones Catholicæ, *rare, but stained and wormed* *Vallisoleti,* 1552
1213 Brigittæ (S.) Revelationes, *portrait* *Antverpiæ,* 1611
1214 Augustini (S.) Opuscula plurima cum Vita a Possidonio conscripta *Argentinæ,* 1489
1215 Collecta Magistralia per Adventum Domini de Formatione Hominis moralis, *Nurembergæ,* 1479—Caraczoli de Licio (R.) Sermones, *ib.* 1479 *in 1 vol.*
1216 Prawa Rousselska: Jus Terrestre Bohemicum, black letter, *very scarce, but wants A i and end of Registrum* *Litomyssl,* 1536

*** The first book printed at Leitomischl.

1217 Prawa Zrizemi Bohemice, *imperfect* *Kralow,* 1564
1218 Avria (V.) Historia chronologica delli Vicere di Sicilia *Palermo,* 1697
1219 Mendez Pinto (Fernan) Peregrinaciones, *wants title* *Madrid,* 1620
1220 Royal Persian Gazette, *odd numbers*
1221 Sesti (G. B.) Piante delle Città, Piazze e Castelli fortificati di Milano, *coloured map and plans, Milano,* 1707 — Ordini pertinenti al Tribunale di Provisione, *ib.* 1657 (2)
1222 Coccinius (M.) de Rebus gestis in Italia (1511-12), *uncut* *Tubingæ,* 1512
1223 Barotti (G. A.) Memorie istoriche di Letterati Ferraresi, vol. I (*all published in this size*), LARGE PAPER, *portraits and vignettes* *Ferrara,* 1777
1224 Neufforge (Sieur de) Recueil élementaire d'Architecture 7 parts in 2 vol. *numerous plates, rare* *Paris,* 1757-65
1225 Parker (G.) on Japaning and Varnishing, *wants plates* *Oxford,* 1688

1226 Turre Rezzonici (A. J. a) ob Minorem Balearium expug-
natam Musarum Epinicia, *frontispiece, Parmæ*, 1557—
De suposititiis militaribus Benedicti Odescalchi qui
Pontifex Maximus, Anno 1676 Innocentii Prænomine
fuit renunciatus, *Comi*, 1742   *in 1 vol.*

1227 Forsyth (W.) Remarks on English Poets, AUTOGRAPH
MS.   1796

1228 Dugdale (Sir W.) Monasticon Anglicanum Epitomized in
English, *plates*   1693

1229 PLAY BILLS of Theatre Royal Covent Garden, from
24 September 1821 to 25 June 1831 inclusive, 10 vol.
1821-31—Drury Lane, from 1 October 1827 to 14 June
1830 inclusive, 3 vol. 1827-30—Haymarket for 1827 and
1828, 2 vol. 1827-28, *half bound*   15 *vol.*

1230 LA FONTAINE (J. DE) FABLES CHOISIES MISES EN
VERS, 4 vol. *portraits of La Fontaine and Oudry, with
beautiful engravings from designs by Oudry, half russia*
Paris, 1755-59

1231 DAFFORNE (J.) MODERN ART, *a series of line engra-
vings from the works of distinguished Painters of the
English and Foreign Schools*, ARTIST'S UNLETTERED
INDIA PROOFS, *half red morocco extra, g. e.*   1877

1232 ARUNDEL SOCIETY'S PLATES. Death of St. Francis,
by D. Ghirlandajo, *finely coloured* — Martyrdom of St.
Sebastian, by P. Perugino, *finely coloured*—Two Fres-
coes, by Ghirlandajo and O. Nelli, *finely coloured, and
18 uncoloured engravings*   (22)

1233 Foxe (J.) Book of Martyrs, black letter, *woodcuts, imperfect*

1234 Book of Common Prayer, black letter, commonly called
" The Sealed Book," *several leaves mended ; sold with
all faults*   1662

1235 Sewell (W.) History of the Quakers   1722

1236 Penn (W.) Works, 2 vol.   1726

1237 Jones (E.) Bardic Museum, *coloured frontispiece by Row-
landson, and Music*   1802

1238 Tacitus translated, with Political Discourses by T. Gor-
don, 2 vol. LARGE PAPER, *old red morocco, g. e.* 1728-31

1239 Le Sage's Historical, Genealogical, Chronological, and
Geographical Atlas, *coloured maps*   1818

1240 Pinkerton (J.) Modern Atlas, 60 *coloured maps, half
bound*   1815

1241 Spenser (E.) Faerie Queene, and other Works, *woodcuts,
calf*   1617

1242 Blagdon's Life of George Morland   *oblong folio.* 1

1243 Album, *bound in white vellum gilt,* containing upwards
of 300 Christmas and New Year's Cards

1244 Shakespeare, Boydell's Graphic Illustrations to, 96 *plates*
(*only*) *after Smirke, Westall, and others, no titles, or
list of plates, one plate torn, and a few stained, calf*
1245 WYATT (M. DIGBY) INDUSTRIAL ARTS OF THE NINE-
TEENTH CENTURY, 116 *highly coloured plates, morocco
extra, gilt, broad gilt sides and edges* 1851
1246 Black's General Atlas, 61 *coloured maps, and Index, half
morocco* *Edinb.* 1851
1247 Music, various, 4 vol. ; &c. (5)
1248 Songs, with pianoforte accompaniments *5 vol.*
1249 Songs (Modern) Dance Music, &c. *a parcel*
1250 Harmonium Museum, by H. Smart, &c. *a parcel*
1251 Piscatoris (J.) Commentarii in Novum Testamentum,
Herbornæ, 1638—Novum Testamentum Græce et duæ
Interpretationes (vetus et nova T. Bezæ) *H. Stephanus,*
1582 (2)
1252 Burkitt (W.) on the New Testament, 1704—Babington
(Bp. G.) Works, 1622—Hooker (R.) Works, *portrait,*
1662—Hall (Bp. J.) Treatises, 1617 (4)
1253 Parliamentary Return, Assurance Companies, 1874;
and others *a parcel*

*The following to the end of the Sale will be sold not
subject to Collation.*

OCTAVO ET INFRA.

1254 Cox (N.) The Gentleman's Recreation, *plates* (*wants the
front.*) 1721—Another Edition; 1674 *2 vol.*
1255 Walton and Cotton, edited by Sir J. Hawkins, *second
edition, plates, calf* (*wants 4 plates*) 1766
1256 Walton and Cotton; *the fourth edition wants 4 plates,* 1792
1257 H. (R.) School of Recreation : or a Guide to Angling,
&c. 1732 (*wants front.*)—Another Edition, 1736 *2 vol.*
1258 Butler (S.) Hudibras, with Annotations by Z. Grey
2 vol. (*wants portrait and plate 9*) *Camb.* 1744—Genuine
Remains, with notes by R. Thyer, 2 vol. 1759 *4 vol.*
1259 Skinner (T.) Life of General Monk, 1723—Sufferings of
Coustos for Free-Masonry, *plates,* 1746 (*wants portrait*)
—Andrews (J. P.) Anecdotes, &c. Ancient and Modern,
1790 *3 vol.*
1260 Comic Latin Grammar (The) *illustrations by J. Leech,*
1840 (*wants pages 11 and 12*)—Caulfield (J.) Chalco-
graphimania, 1814 ; and another *3 vol.*
1261 More (Sir Thos.) Commonwealth of Utopia, *frontispiece
by Marshall,* 1639 (*wants pages 81 to 88*) ; &c. *6 vol.*

QUARTO.

1262 Augustini (S.) Sermones, 2 vol. *black letter, woodcut
initials (vol. II wants folio* CLXXVII)
Lugd. J. Mareschal, 1520

1263 Life and Reign of Queen Elizabeth, also the Trial and
Death of Mary Queen of Scots, *portraits, &c. (wants
pages 205 to 208)* 1738—Dalforne (R.) The Appren-
tice's Time-Entertainer accomptantly, 1640   *2 vol.*

1264 Ames (J.) Typographical Antiquities, *woodcuts, calf
(wants a plate at page 79)*   1749

FOLIO.

1265 Knolles (R.) Historie of the Turkes, *woodcut portraits,
half calf,* 1603—Aristotle's Politiques, by L. Le Roy,
2 vol. (*wants pages 225 to 228*) 1598

1266 Sandford (F.) Genealogical History of the Kings of
England and Monarchs of Great Britain, *numerous
plates, calf (wants pages 299 to 302)*   1677
  ₊ Contains the autograph of Sir Robert Southwell, Clerk
of the Privy Council to Charles II.

END OF SALE.

Dryden Press: J. Davy and Sons, 137, Long Acre, London.